HOW TO MAKE

MODEL AIRCRAFT

CHRIS ELLIS

Arco Publishing Company, Inc.
New York

Published by Arco Publishing Company, Inc.
219 Park Avenue South, New York, N.Y. 10003

Copyright © 1974 The Hamlyn Publishing Group Limited

Library of Congress Catalog Card Number 73-92268
ISBN 0-668-03448-3

Printed in Great Britain

Contents

Acknowledgments

Illustrating this book would have been impossible without the kind and willing help of a good number of friends and fellow enthusiasts. The model aircraft hobby has so many ramifications that it would be almost impossible for any one person to experience personally every aspect of it. For instance I have never made a 1:24 scale model for the simple reason that I don't have room for anything that big! So I'm dependent on someone who has been involved in this sort of model for the loan of pictures (plus a few comments on the subject in passing). There are other scales or types of model which I've only briefly experienced, so to get a comprehensive coverage for the reader of this book I've borrowed pictures from specialists in various subjects within the model aircraft hobby. In addition to all the manufacturers mentioned by name throughout the text I wish to thank Bryan Fosten, Les Whitehouse, Gerald Scarborough, Mihail Moisecu, Michael Andress, Peter Halliday, Jerry Scutts, Alan H. Butler, Gordon Stevens, Richard M. Goldman, Don Spering, M. Brunon, Paul Camelio, C. J. Attard, Mike Gething, Richard E. Gardner, Tony Woollett, Fred Henderson, Harry Woodman, Philip Stearns, and Keith Palmer. Photographs used in the text are acknowledged individually; those not acknowledged belong to the author. J. Groeneveld very kindly supplied several pictures specially for this book and also provided details of how to take them. One picture is taken from the Japanese publication *Model Art*. Philip Stearns took all the colour photographs which are not otherwise credited. Finally I must thank Sue Boyd for typing the bulk of the manuscript.

1 : Model Aircraft as a Hobby

Of all constructional hobbies, making model aircraft is one of the most familiar, as plastic kits are sold in virtually every town and city. This book is intended to serve as a guide for anyone starting out to make up scale model aircraft and the idea is to show that there is considerably more potential to the craft than simply assembling models straight out of the kit. Even those with some experience should find plenty to interest them within these pages, and I should explain that we are here considering static display models rather than models of the flying variety which belong to a different hobby altogether!

Plastic aircraft assembly kits greatly outnumber all other types of plastic kit produced, and though many hundreds of kits have appeared in the last two decades there is little sign of a slackening in either demand or output. The number of plastic model aircraft enthusiasts appears to grow from year to year, and virtually everybody starts off by purchasing these readily available plastic kits. Relative to other hobbies, model aircraft are very cheap; few other hobbies can still be financed if needs be at no more than true 'pocket money' prices, though there are kits at the upper end of the price range which cost as much as a model train set if you have that sort of money to spend.

New kits appear virtually every month and some manufacturers are very prolific indeed. The choice facing the purchaser is huge and it would be virtually impossible for any one individual to make up every kit on the market. With so many kits available most modellers never have any inclination or need to move on from plastic kits and this book concentrates mainly on these. It is possible to move on from plastic kit building to rather more complicated 'semi' kits, and even scratch building from raw materials. I've included a chapter in this book which shows the possibilities in this direction.

In the days when wood was the commonest material used for scale model aircraft it was fashionable to look down on plastic kits as being an inferior way to make models. The plastic kit, however, soon eclipsed the wooden construction kit which rapidly disappeared from the scene in the late 1950s. It was soon acknowledged that the plastic kit model had a lot of new virtues. For a start it took the sheer drudgery out of model aircraft building; in the days of wooden kits many hours had to be spent simply sanding and carving wings and fuselage to shape and contour. This was the major part of the exercise and it dominated the task at the expense – in most cases – of true scale fidelity of finish and markings. In those days the average modeller seemed happy enough to arrive at a Spitfire which actually looked like a Spitfire, and the finer points of camouflage pattern and squadron markings were often forgotten – or at best were glossed over.

In a plastic kit the drudgery is done for you – the fuselage, wings, and other parts come ready shaped and finely detailed. The 'fun' part of the operation becomes assembly and finishing, the most interesting of modelling activities, and this becomes the major part of the work. Also, given the basic airframe shape you can embark on the other interesting activities of adding extra detail or converting the model to depict something other than the manufacturer intended. And if your efforts result in failure you have the satisfaction of knowing that you have not wasted too much money.

With a craft knife, some cement, and a kit you are in the model aircraft business. Clearly it is the ease with which you can get started, plus the low initial outlay, which has made model aircraft construction from kits such a popular pastime. Thousands who happily cement parts together and execute intricate paint schemes on plastic models would never have dreamed of getting started if wooden kits were still the only ones around. So plastic kits have put model aircraft within the reach of all, and there is now a choice to please everyone with an interest in aviation. When you start making model aircraft you cannot avoid getting to know more about avionics and aviation history. And if that does not inspire you, the hobby can still be more than justified by its relaxation value – getting involved in making a scale model is a great escape from everyday life.

Before proceeding further I would like to mention here the International Plastic Modelling Society (IPMS) which exists to serve the enthusiastic modeller and has branches in most countries of the Western World. This organization produces journals and organizes many meets and competitions where you can see the very best standards of modelling. Membership details are given in most hobby periodicals.

Finally, a handy little book to have is *Plastic Kits of the World*, published by Model and Aeronautical Press. This tabulates all kits ever produced together with details of scales and makers.

1 One of the most intricate of modern kits is the Hasegawa 1 : 32 scale model of the Sabre jet. It includes moving control surfaces, sliding cockpit cover, opening air-brakes, detailed gunbays, and a fully detailed removable engine (Jerry Scutts).

2 : Scales

Scale is a crucial aspect of all modelling activities, for the scale determines the size of a model and may affect the complexity, price, and availability of any given range of kits. By 'scale' we mean the size of the model relative to the size of the real life original. Thus an airliner model might be a hundred times smaller than the actual aircraft. It would be known as a 1/100 scale model. Put in another way the model would be smaller than the actual aircraft by a ratio of 1:100 – or 1 inch on the model would be equal to 100 inches on the real aircraft. You will see the scale quoted by the model manufacturer in either of these forms – 1/100 or 1:100. Similarly a model quoted as 1/24 or 1:24 scale will be 24 times smaller than its original. In this particular case it can be seen quite readily that $\frac{1}{2}$ inch on the model is equal to 1 foot (12 inches) on the real thing. Sometimes you may see a model quoted as being, say, $\frac{1}{4}$ inch to 1 foot scale rather than being expressed in fractional terms. Hence a modest amount of mental arithmetic may be needed to find out the scale in fractional terms; in the example given here, $\frac{1}{4}$ inch to 1 foot (12 inches) obviously means that the model would be to 1/48 or 1:48 scale. When model aircraft first appeared there was hardly such a thing as an ordered series of scales. The maker chose some arbitrary size for the model, usually quite big. By the 1920s, if not earlier, those models which were appearing in kit form – often in cardboard – were being produced to recognizable scales; 1:24 was an early and obvious choice. When a kit maker made a range of models it was sensible to keep to the same scale throughout so that, say, as many as six kits might be available all in 1:24 scale. The enthusiast who constructed all six would end up with six models all bearing the same relationship to each other in terms of size as the originals. This idea of 'constant scale' has always remained popular and a collection of models all to the same scale is quite obviously instructive as well as merely

being amusing and convenient. It can be seen instantly how much bigger a bomber is than a fighter plane, for instance. In a collection of models which spans a long period of time (in full-size terms) it is interesting just to see how the size and design of such types as fighter aircraft have increased and developed over the years – compare a Sopwith Camel, Spitfire, P-47 Thunderbolt, and a Phantom jet, for instance, to see at a glance the unbelievable increase in size over the 60 years spanned by the originals. In fact, the same sort of size comparison would be much more difficult with actual aircraft, even supposing you had the chance to get them together!

In the early 1930s the idea of collecting model aircraft to a constant scale got a major boost from the Skybirds range, which pioneered the idea of the small scale assembly kit. James Hay Stevens, the Skybirds designer, chose a scale of 1:72 (1 inch to 6 feet) which roughly matched the scale of contemporary small model cars. This compact 1:72 scale kept the model to a very handy size, and the price quite reasonable, so it became instantly popular. Other kit makers followed this size and the early Frog Penguin plastic kits (which appeared in 1938) were also 1:72 scale. In Britain, in particular, 1:72 scale has been the major 'constant scale' for model aircraft ever since the original Skybirds kits appeared. Elsewhere, however, different manufacturers tended to go their own ways and it is only in the last decade that almost all kit manufacturers have standardized on 1:72 scale for their main model aircraft kit output. Thus 1:72 scale is the most popular of all standard scales for model aircraft and is likely to remain so.

In the last few years, however, with nearly all the best known aircraft types already available in 1:72 scale, the kit makers have tended to exploit a variety of new scales. This has led recently to a prolific increase in the number of new kits appearing in these 'new' sizes. Small kits in 1:144 scale (half the size of 1:72), and 1:100 scale are appearing in increasing numbers. While at the other end of the market some huge and beautifully detailed kits in 1:32, 1:24, and 1:20 scales have been produced. With such a choice of scales now available, however, the

1 A graphic demonstration of the difference in scale sizes is afforded by this view of the 1:32 scale Hasegawa Grumman Hellcat (centre) flanked by 1:72 scale versions by Frog and Airfix. Note the hinged control surfaces on the 1:32 scale model, working detail made possible by the big size. The Airfix model (nearest) has hinged ailerons, even in 1:72 scale (Jerry Scutts).

2 A constant scale collection – this one is to 1:72 scale – shows a fascinating comparison in size between aircraft types. Add variations in colour scheme and the whole lot makes an impressive line-up. Theme of this collection is Allied aircraft of the Second World War (J. Groeneveld).

3 The beautiful quality of a 1:24 scale model is seen in this view of the Airfix Messerschmitt B 109E made by Gerald Scarborough. Note the very smooth finish, the fine detail added, and the movable control surface. The cowling panels are removable and are slightly disturbed in this view. This model has a new finish and markings applied not featured in the kit.

4 Though 1:48 scale is relatively small, recent kits incorporate much fine detail. Tamiya's Rufe has a sliding canopy and a launching cradle, plus pilot and other features.

modeller is faced with the task of settling on just what to collect and it will be helpful to look at each of the main scales in more detail to assess their potential.

1:72 Scale

As related above this is by far the most popular of all plastic scale model aircraft scales and as much as 90 per cent of the market is geared to this size. Major manufacturers in Britain, USA, Japan, France, Czechoslovakia, and Germany have all produced the bulk of their output in 1:72. Most of the 'accessory' market also caters for this scale – thus there are decal sheets, conversion parts, structures, figures, vehicles, and so on all available to match the kits, and most aircraft drawings published in specialist magazines are also to 1:72 scale, making reference work from these drawings an easy matter. Prices for small aircraft in this scale start in the 'pocket money' range and the choice of subject is huge. Hundreds of different kits are available at any one time though only the very largest hobby stores will stock more than a selection of them. Suffice to say that this scale is the one for

the modeller who wishes to build up a big collection. The choice of subject is so big in fact that few modellers would have time to make all the kits available. Even so there are several well-known private collections with over 1,000 models in them. Thus it is possible to assemble a veritable miniature museum of aircraft history, and the relative cheapness and availability of 1:72 scale kits also means that even more aircraft types can be depicted by conversion or alteration of basic kits. The choice is so vast, in fact, that many modellers who collect in 1:72 scale now specialize in certain types of aircraft rather than collect all types at random. For instance one could collect naval aircraft, fighters, bombers, aircraft of the First World War, light civilian aircraft, and so on. The choice of subject for this sort of sub-specialization is almost limitless. Some modellers go in for more than one sub-group – for example aircraft of the First World War and aircraft of the Second World War. Some enthusiasts go in for single 'types' or makes, especially those which were prolific and famous in aviation history; thus it is possible to collect models of the Spitfire in all its many forms and variations, not to say colour schemes and squadron markings.

The main advantage of 1:72 scale, aside from wide scope, availability, and low price, is, of course, compactness, while a high degree of fine detail can be (and is) achieved.

1:48 Scale

Back in the 1930s this was quite a popular scale for wood models. In the age of plastic kits it has retained its popularity, more among modellers it seems than manufacturers. For though several kit makers offer a limited number of 1:48 scale kits, the total number of types available in kit form at any one time is probably less than fifty and only the larger hobby stores stock them. At ¼ inch to 1 foot the size of any given model is substantially bigger than the 1:72 scale equivalent. This allows the inclusion of true 'super detail' features like operating control surfaces, folding wings in naval aircraft, bomb hoists, and the like. If these features are not actually included with the kit it is easy enough to add them. Aurora, Monogram, Revell, and Tamiya all produce some kits in 1:48. Aurora's range includes some very early examples of their output in this scale with such classic types as the Boeing P-26 'Peashooter' and the Curtiss Helldiver – mostly very good models when it is considered that the moulds are approaching 20 years old. Because of their size nothing bigger than a twin-engine machine seems to have been produced in 1:48 scale, Revell's B-25 Mitchell being the biggest I can recall. 1:48 scale has a few side advantages in that it matches closely the scale of O gauge railways. Thus various figures, die-cast cars, and other accessories are available in this scale which facilitates scenic display of the models.

In Japan and Italy a few model aircraft kits have been produced to 1:50 scale. This is so close to 1:48 as to make no appreciable visual difference in size and most modellers freely mix 1:48 and 1:50 scale.

1:32 Scale

This is one of the 'newer' scales which has found favour in recent years. Revell initiated the idea

with some classic fighters of the Second World War; the idea was extremely well received and there is now a small but steady flow of kits to this scale – including some twin-engine types – with some Japanese kit makers also producing to the same scale. In linear terms, 1:32 scale is ⅜ inch to 1 foot; it matches the popular 54 mm scale model soldier size and is also the scale adopted for many car kits, so there are plenty of accessories available for scenic display. The aircraft in this scale are made from superbly detailed mouldings, usually with excellent intricate dummy engines and other internal fittings. It is not difficult to add even more detail in this large size and most models so far produced have been very accurate, with only occasional lapses in some early kit offerings. Space, or lack of it, is likely to be your major limitation in this scale. A model covers the shelf area of about four 1:72 scale models.

1:24 Scale (and 1:20)

Airfix went even bigger than Revell when they produced a Spitfire kit in 1:24 scale in 1970. At ½ inch to 1 foot, models in this scale are very big and impressive. Airfix have provided nearly all the detail both outside and inside on the kits so far released, with a very well hidden electric motor which drives the propeller. One or two Japanese kit makers have come up with similar style models, often in 1:20 scale. As most 1:20 scale models depict light aircraft the size works out about the size of 1:24 scale. The kits available at the time of writing are few in number and

6 Though difficult to believe, this Buccaneer is in the small 1:100 scale series put out by Tamiya. The picture is actually reproduced to a larger size than the little model really is.

the models take up a lot of space. They take longer to make than smaller less complex models and need more care and concentration, for what might be a tiny and almost unnoticeable painting blemish on a 1:72 scale model will stand out vastly magnified in 1:32 scale. Everything is scaled up – even constructional problems; because of the extra weight involved it takes more care and skill to get wings to the correct dihedral than it would in 1:72 scale. Nothing can be skimped; strictly speaking there should be no short cuts in any scale but anything much short of perfection in 1:24 scale will produce an unsatisfactory model. I would not recommend this scale for the complete novice – get some experience in 1:72 or 1:48 scale first.

1:100 Scale

Very conveniently this works out at 3 mm to 1 foot, so measurements are easy to transfer from full-size to model dimensions. Faller of West Germany originated the scale in the 1950s as far as model aircraft are concerned. Their range was still available at the time of writing and depicts Second World War and post-war German service and civil aircraft. For a long

period the scale was dormant, but Tamiya revived the scale a few years ago with some superbly moulded kits of military jets and helicopters. These are, in fact, among the best of all kits on the market as far as accuracy, presentation, and detail is concerned. Being about 30 per cent smaller all round than 1:72 scale, these models offer compactness with absolutely no sacrifice in detail.

If storage or display space is your problem this scale is worth considering. The models available are very satisfying and the prices are modest. Faller models, being older, do not come up to Tamiya's standard of moulding, and there are some inaccuracies too which need correcting. A few other makers produce odd kits in 1:100 scale, among them Heller. Taken together the 1:100 scale kits available offer a reasonable choice of subject with the range always increasing.

1:144 Scale

Exactly half the linear size of 1:72 scale, and only a quarter the size by volume, this is another scale which has seen a recent revival. For many years Airfix and some other makers have offered a few airliner kits in 1:144 scale. In 1973, however, Revell produced a large range of fighters and attack aircraft covering British, American, German, and Japanese subjects of the Second

World War. Otaki, a Japanese manufacturer, joined in with some fighters and twin-engined bombers, and a 'new' scale was born almost overnight. These 1:144 scale models (12 feet to 1 inch) are really tiny – two fighters sit comfortably on the palm of the hand – and their availability means that even those enthusiasts who did not previously collect models due to lack of space now have no excuse for not starting! For anyone living in a pint-sized apartment, 1:144 scale is the answer. Twelve or so models will easily fit in a shoebox, or a small shelf could hold an entire collection.

In 1:144 scale you do not, of course, get fine detail, in the sense that tiny parts like D/F loops are usually omitted, though they would barely be visible anyway in this small size. The moulding quality is generally good, and construction is usually quite simple. But you can add a lot of detail yourself; for example I have added cockpit interiors to some of mine. Markings and painting details left a little to be desired on the early kits I have made up, but these will no doubt improve. 1:144 scale models need careful painting, much of the work being of a delicate nature, if they are not to look clumsy.

Aside from small size, low 'pocket money' price, and fair simplicity, these 1:144 scale miniatures have a charm of their own and make a pleasant diversion from working in the larger scales. On the scenic side remember that N gauge model railway accessories (1:148–1:160 scale) like personnel, trucks, buildings, and stores, are ideal for use with 1:144 scale model aircraft. An airfield diorama scene would need only a card table to give a realistic area for display or photography in this size.

Other Models

Though all the scales mentioned here refer to kits in some form or other, do not overlook your local toyshop for some ready made 'toys' with big model potential. There are several ranges to be seen where the models are quite acceptable with a little working up, after which they can be added to a series of kit built models. For instance, Bachmann have a large range of 'Miniplanes', all moulded in hard plastic and mostly accurate and well detailed. They are to no set scales but some are close to 1:144, others to 1:100, so they can be modified and added to a collection made from kits. Edison is an Italian firm making die-cast 1:72 scale aircraft, some of them, like the Sopwith Baby, not otherwise available in kit form. With some added detail

7 Also to 1:100 scale by Tamiya is the Sky Crane, complete with hoist and stores module. It is so well detailed that the scale is difficult to estimate with no available size comparison. Rotor head detail is worthy of note.

and a good repaint these can be transformed into reasonable additions to a collection. Finally, watch for breakfast cereal premiums and the like. Sometimes they include aircraft in kit form.

Scale Compatibility

It can be seen that aircraft models come in distinct size and scale categories, and most models sold in kit form fall into one or the other groups. There are still numerous old kits on sale where slightly odd scales are encountered. Similarly odd accessories crop up to slightly unusual scales. In practice, however, if your collection is to 1:72 scale, model airplanes between about 1:69 and 1:76 scale will not look out of place grouped with the 1:72 scale pieces. It would take a measuring session with a ruler for the 'odd scale' models to be detected. Similarly 1:96 scale models (of which a few are available) will go happily with 1:100 scale models. And so it goes on. Do not be put off, therefore, by what appears to be an unusual scale. Years ago Frog made the classic Dragon Rapide in 1:67 scale (it is long out of production), but this has for years been the nearest there is to a 1:72 scale version, and the model can be seen in many collections of nominally 1:72 scale aircraft. In short, if a model is very close to a recognized scale it will generally be compatible visually.

3: Basic Tools and Materials

Plastic model aircraft can be made quite satisfactorily using only the most basic tools and materials though there is, of course, no limit to how much you spend on a tool kit. Below are some of the tools and materials which I commend for the average modeller. Hobby shops usually carry a reasonable choice of tools and there are several well-known ranges including X-acto, Multicraft and Swann and Morton.

Much of the work in kit assembly consists of cutting, filing and smoothing the plastic parts. Various types of craft knife are available, the blades in all cases being replaceable and there is usually a choice of blades to fit each handle. It is a good idea always to have at least one complete set of new blades. This means that a replacement is available instantly if any blade breaks or becomes blunt so there will be no hold-up in any modelling work. Good sharp blades are needed for the most intricate cutting and cleaning-up work. Older blunter blades should be conserved as they are frequently useful for scraping or 'rough work'. Keep all blades in a small tin for safety's sake, especially if there are small children or pet animals in the house. It is a good idea to have more than one tin – one for new sharp blades and one for older ones. Also needed is a cutting board – essential both for good work and for protecting the furniture. A square of formica, a thermo-plastic tile, a

1 The most basic model-making requirements are shown here – large and small craft knives, small file, and fine glasspaper (*top centre*), together with tweezers, spare blades, razor saw, dividers, steel rule, small drills, and fine wire. Also shown are lead weights and body putty.

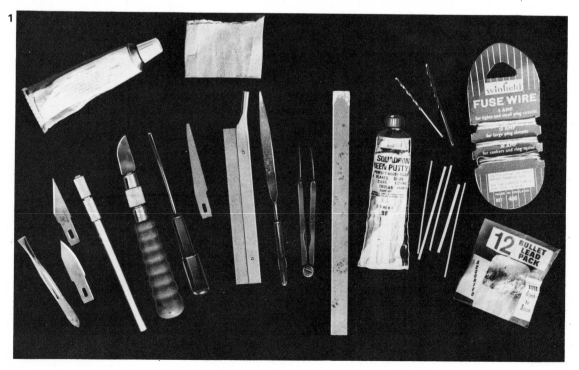

small glass sheet or similar hard flat surface is commended. A steel rule is essential as an edge for cutting plastic sheet or tape, as well as in its usual role as a measuring aid. The other cutting instrument of value is a razor-saw, used for almost all conversion work and heavy duty cutting. It is, in effect, a miniature tenon saw with very fine teeth and it well repays the modest outlay involved in its purchase.

Various tools and items are needed to clean up edges and surfaces during assembly or conversion work. Small round files, sometimes known as 'rat-tail' files, are sold at the larger hobby stores or can be had from some engineering suppliers. These are usually pointed and are invaluable for such chores as opening up radiator intakes and thinning the lips of cowlings, etc. Small flat files are similarly available. A selection of small 'pin' drills (also sold by big hobby stores) is a necessity. These very fine drills can be operated simply by rotating them in the fingers. I find though a chuck and handle can be used to hold the drill if desired. This sort of drill is useful for piercing rigging holes, opening out gun barrels, and so on. Further useful items are an emery board (sold in chain stores) and a selection of fine glass papers and 'wet and dry' paper. Wire wool or the domestic abrasive 'Duraglit' is another item sometimes used. The latter, in particular used sparingly, is very good for polishing out unwanted scratch marks on the plastic surface. Additional types of cement are very useful – I always have 'Five Minute Epoxy' handy (sold under various brand names) and some sort of 'Universal' type glue like Uhu. These adhesives are useful for cementing otherwise non-compatible materials. For example, you may at some stage wish to cement a wood radiator to a plastic wing.

Clear adhesive tape, rubber bands, or clothes pegs are all useful items for holding parts together while the cement sets.

The foregoing covers a basic outfit of essentials (or near essentials at least) and should give the average modeller a good set of working tools and materials. You can get by on less – just a knife and a tube of cement for starters – but sooner or later you will have a need for the other items. In addition to the above there is a use for normal domestic tools already found in most homes. These include tweezers (for holding small parts), small pliers, set square, plastic ruler, pencil, etc.

Unless you have a workbench in den or workroom, you will also need some sort of working surface. An old drawing board or a wooden tray is ideal. All your modelling work can be done on the board which can then be placed wherever you are working. This means that you will not be working directly on such furnishings as the dining table or sideboard – cuts or cement smears on the furniture are not very popular in the average household! Plastic aircraft modelling can be enjoyed in the living room if adequate precautions are taken. Put old newspaper under your board if you are modelling on the dining table.

All the tools and materials so far described and illustrated can be purchased as individual items and most of them are still in or near the 'pocket money' class, even after the price increases of recent years.

If your means are limited you can purchase these items one piece at a time, starting with a cheap craft knife and acquiring the more specialized tools as time goes by. For the most basic kit building you need only a small set of essential tools. Where finance is not a limiting factor there is nothing to stop you acquiring a fine set of modelling tools in one go by purchasing one or other of the 'de luxe' tool chests which are sold by the larger hobby stores. A typical range by Multicraft is shown on the next page. There is a single knife with spare blades in a handy pocket wallet, then three wood tool chests, each with plush nested interior for the various tools. As can be seen the largest set provides three knife handles, every possible blade and router shape, a small hacksaw, a small razor-saw blade, files, and even a grindstone for re-sharpening the blades. The most useful knife blades are the straight edge or curved shapes, the latter being the best for general work.

Yet further 'luxury' tools can be acquired. For example there are several small jeweller's vices available, miniatures of the more commonly seen types of vice. Some have adjustable or pivoted heads for working at any desired angle. As precision instruments they are rather expensive. There are some small vices specially made for modellers – the MiniVice range is the best known of these. In practice such an item is definitely a luxury rather than a necessity. The same may be said of D clamps and surgeon's scalpels – sold by medical suppliers – which are really more expensive equivalents of the clothes peg and craft knife. (Jewellers' suppliers and stamp shops sell various types of magnifying stands which, again, may be useful when it comes to fine detail work or painting.)

There are some excellent small power drills available and at least one comes as part of a versatile system which provides a stand and other fittings. A power drill is not really essential for plastic kit work, however.

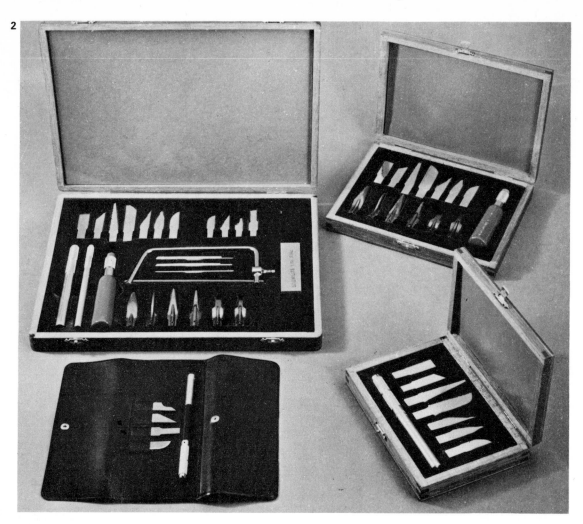

Materials

So far we have been concerned with a basic range of working tools and materials. For convenience we can now look at some essential constructional materials which will be needed subsequently, especially if you make models on an ambitious scale. Examples later in the book will show some of these things in use. There is no need to acquire all of them in advance, but read about them now and then start looking.

Plastic Card

Sold under various trade names (examples Polycard, Plastiboard, Rikokard), this material looks like ordinary card but is, in fact, polystyrene in sheet form. It comes in handy size packs or as single sheets. Some makers offer colours like black, blue, red, or yellow, but white is the most common. Some makers also produce transparent sheets of plastic card. The range of

sizes available is well shown in the illustration. This is the list of thicknesses and sizes of plastic card put out by one British firm under the Riko name and is typical of several other ranges. The table is printed on plastic card. Plastic card sheets, it can be seen, come in varying thicknesses and are measured in thousandths of an inch or in millimetres. The most useful thicknesses are 10 thou, 20 thou, 30 thou, and 40 thou (thou = thousandths of an inch) or the metric equivalents. Most plastic card is matt finished and can take pen or pencil marks, so that shapes can be drawn up before cutting out.

The properties of plastic card are like those of all polystyrene in that the material can be glued with polystyrene cement (or liquid cement). It is also affected by heat. For example if plastic card is curved round a former and bound it can be held in hot water and will take up the new shape permanently – useful for making curved panels on models. The card is stiff enough for all normal handling and it is usually cut by using a

2 Some typical complete tool sets.

3 Sample sheet giving plastic card sizes from typical supplier.

RIKO regd.

RICHARD KOHNSTAM LIMITED

13-15A HIGH STREET, HEMEL HEMPSTEAD, HERTFORDSHIRE

POLYSTYRENE SHEET

R.0358	.125mm	White
R.0340	.25mm	White
R.0359	.375mm	White
R.0341	.5mm	White
R.0342	.5mm	Black
R.0349	.75mm	White
R.0350	.75mm	Black
R.0351	1mm	White
R.0352	1mm	Black
R.0353	1.5mm	White
R.0354	1.5mm	Black
R.0355	.25mm	Clear
R.0356	.5mm	Clear
R.0357	Assorted Colours	
	.5mm	Red
	.5mm	Cream
	.5mm	Yellow
	.5mm	Green
	.5mm	Light Blue
	.5mm	Dark Blue

POLYSTYRENE MINISTRIP

White
R.0360	.125mm	x 1, 1.5 & 2mm
R.0361	.25mm	x 1, 1.5 & 2mm
R.0362	.5mm	x 1, 1.5 & 2mm
R.0363	.5mm	x .5mm
R.0364	.5mm	x .75mm
R.0365	.5mm	x 1mm
R.0366	.5mm	x 1.5mm
R.0367	.5mm	x 2mm

Assorted Colours
R.0390	.5mm	x .5mm
R.0391	.5mm	x .75mm
R.0392	.5mm	x 1mm
R.0393	.5mm	x 1.5mm
R.0394	.5mm	x 2mm

POLYSTYRENE ROD

R.0395	.75mm	Diameter
R.0396	1mm	Diameter
R.0397	1.25mm	Diameter

POLYSTYRENE BUILDING SHEET

OO/HO 4mm scale

S.0370	Red Brick		S.0372	Grey Slate
S.0371	Yellow Brick		S.0373	Road Signs

Printed on R.0341

craft knife and a straight edge steel rule. The technique is to score along the cut line, then simply snap it off cleanly. Scissors can also be used for cutting plastic card, a handy point to remember when complex curved shapes are required.

Plastic card is one of the most versatile of all modelling materials. Advanced modellers actually build complete finely detailed replicas of aircraft from plastic card, though this is an art in itself beyond the scope of this book. For those who mainly build aircraft from kits the material has dozens of uses. For example, the wheel well doors on many small plastic models are well over scale thickness as supplied in moulded form. It is quite common practice to replace the kit doors with thin replicas cut from plastic card, using the original doors as templates. New wingtips, tailplanes, cockpit floors, instrument consoles, radiator flaps, and other small parts all provide opportunities for using plastic card. Examples of the material in use are shown elsewhere in the book.

Plastic Card Strip (or Polystyrene Strip)

This is simply plastic card sheeting sliced into fine strips by the suppliers and sold in various combinations of width or thickness. Widths are from about 0.5 mm up to 2–3 mm. The Riko listing is typical, their particular brand name being Ministrip; Microstrip is another well-known name. Depending upon the scale of your model, polystyrene strip has unlimited uses – from interplane struts to radiator intake louvres. On large scale models it is used for cockpit canopy framing, on others it can be used to depict stringers for internal detailing, and so on.

In very small models a length of strip may well make a scale size aileron. A selection of packs of this useful material is a commended addition to your list of supplies.

Polystyrene Rod

Thin diameter plastic rod is another product in plastic and this also comes in assorted sizes – as shown with the plastic card list. For aircraft models this material is used – for example – to fashion exhaust pipes, struts, or oleo legs among other things. If you are doing much detail or conversion work then plastic rod is a desirable acquisition.

Building Sheet

As can be seen from the Riko list there is also a selection of so-called 'building sheets' which are simply polystyrene sheet moulded or embossed with brick or stone pattern, etc., as listed. While of little direct value for aircraft modelling, this material is worth using for scenic work in a display – as, for instance, when making model buildings for a miniature airfield scene.

Plastic Sprue and Spare Parts

The left-over pieces from a completed kit are themselves of some value to the aircraft modeller. Many kits these days include optional parts, allowing the model to be made up in one of, perhaps, two or three different forms. Thus there may be two optional engine types, two different nose mouldings, and so on. Any parts not used should be kept as they will almost certainly find a place in some later model project. For example, in the Sea Hornet night-fighter conversion illustrated on another page, the nose radome was cut and fashioned from the front end of a torpedo which was left over from another kit. The 'sprues' or 'runners' which hold the moulded parts together should also be retained, especially the straight long lengths. Odd pieces come in handy for reinforcement work in conversions, while when drawn into fine filaments (by softening and pulling them over a heat source as described later), these sprues are usable for everything from rigging wires to exhaust pipes.

Other Pieces

Lastly there is always a need for oddments of everyday material, and modelling clay, small metal weights (as are sold in fishermen's supply shops), fuse wire, fine copper wire, and any odd items that can be utilized – plastic cocktail sticks are an example.

Storage

The key to speedy conversion and detail work is to have a good storage system so that any requisite item or spare part can be located very quickly.

I have a transparent plastic filing folder in which to keep an assortment of polystyrene sheets, and this also makes a convenient place to keep rulers and set squares. An old kit box – clearly labelled – is useful for storing sliced polystyrene sheet (e.g. Ministrip or Microstrip) offcuts, and also for plastic rod, old cocktail sticks, or other scrap items of possible modelling potential. For spare parts there is a type of small workshop cabinet made in transparent plastic and sold quite cheaply in chain stores. It has several small drawers and compartments so that, for example, propellers can be kept in one section, wheels in another, and so on. The alternative is to use a transparent plastic food container – or more than one. The 'see-through' nature of these items is helpful, for available stock can be seen at a glance without the need for sifting through handfuls of pieces taken out of an old cardboard box. Tools are best kept in another box. An old kit box would do but I find a metal box more convenient, especially from the safety angle. With a cheap metal box there is no danger of a knife blade piercing the container, a point to remember if there are young children nearby. With everything boxed (and the boxes labelled), the various necessities for successful kit making can be stowed away quickly and relatively unobtrusively at the end of a modelling session.

4: Research and References

One of the most important aspects of successful aircraft modelling does not involve any actual constructional work at all. Like most hobbies, the satisfaction you get from making model aircraft can be greatly affected by the work you put into it. Taking a very obvious analogy, look at stamp collecting. A basic way of going about it is to purchase random packets of stamps, remove others from envelopes, and mount the lot haphazardly into an album, maybe pausing only to group the stamps by countries. This gives you a collection of sorts, but not a very interesting one, and one moreover with a very limited chance of retaining your interest for long. However, once you purchase a stamp catalogue and read some magazines and articles on the subject, you begin to discover that there is more to the hobby than was at first obvious. The stamps can be sorted out into issues, and sets, and all sorts of other variations become important, like perforations and watermarks. Some study of the literature of the hobby enables you to group your stamps by sets and then find out any other individual stamps you need to complete a set – and so on. In other words, whether consciously or not, you have done some research and it has greatly enhanced the enjoyment and interest you can get from the pastime.

The model aircraft hobby is almost exactly like this. You can call in at any hobby store and purchase a plastic aircraft kit at random, then take it home and assemble it following the kit instructions. Paint it and apply the markings from the kit and that is about as far as you can go if you depend solely on the kit contents for inspiration. Many young modellers do just this when they first make up model aircraft; very often the model never reaches the painting stage and it does little more than gather dust, sustain superficial damage and then eventually get thrown away, only to be replaced by another model with a similarly short 'life'. At this stage the novice to model aircraft building is in the same haphazard position as a novice stamp collector. So where does he go from here? Well the simple answer, as with the embryo stamp collector, is to study the subject.

Reading this book for the first time, the chances are that you are already familiar with specialist aviation or modelling magazines; you will almost certainly have seen them on a news-stand even if you are not already a reader. Similarly you will be aware that there is a seemingly endless flow of aviation books, including numerous reference works which give technical details and histories of aircraft types. Most public libraries seem to have at least one shelf of nothing but aviation books, so whatever your financial resources there is usually some way, either by purchase or by borrowing, by which you can get hold of books and periodicals.

In my experience most model aircraft collectors were aviation enthusiasts long before they became modellers and as real aircraft are very much part of the modern everyday environment, in most parts of the world, the majority of aviation enthusiasts get interested in the subject at an early age. Certainly in my case, it was an absorbing interest in real aircraft which started me off on making models.

What this boils down to is that your own knowledge of the subject, either latent or actual, will enable you to get much more out of a kit of parts than is apparent on first consideration. To illustrate this, take the famous German Messerschmitt 109 fighter, which in various scales is a popular subject for virtually all kit manufacturers. You decide to buy a kit, having settled which scale to choose. If you have studied the various hobby magazines, you may well have read reviews of the various Messerschmitt 109 kits on the market and you will have an impression of which kit you wish to purchase.

Having acquired the Me 109 kit, what can be done with it? Resist the first impulse to cement all the parts together as soon as you open the box. Instead, spend at least an evening, if not longer, studying its potential. You may already have a good knowledge about Me 109s in general – you may be quite unfamiliar with it. Whichever way it is with you, turn up all the reference material you can find on the Me 109. There have been countless magazine articles over the years, there is a Profile, and at least four complete books on the Messerschmitt 109 are known to me. In addition the Me 109 is covered in virtually all books dealing with Luftwaffe aircraft. So either from your own collection, the public library, or from friends, you must be able to find some assorted literature. Read this, make any notes of salient facts about the aircraft and study the kit parts against any photos or plans in your reference material. If you have access to any magazine reviews of the kit in question see what they have to say; these reviews often point out any errors in the kit itself (e.g.: fin and rudder misshapen) and such errors need correcting when the model is assembled. If you can find no reviews, then you will need to measure and judge accuracy for yourself, using the reference material you have available. Use this research period to appreciate the character of the aircraft in your own imagination. Whether or not you realize it, imagination plays a big part in model making. It probably persuaded you to buy the kit in the first place – not for nothing do the kit manufacturers put fine 'action' illustrations on the box lids – and use of your imagination at this stage will help formulate your approach to the model. It helps, for instance, if you can 'see' the finished model in full-size terms in the conditions of the time. If you have a picture of the actual aircraft – I much prefer to model specific machines which are recorded pictorially in books or magazines – study the detail in the pictures very carefully. Look for fresh or worn paintwork, and small stencilling. Are the ailerons 'drooping'?, is the cockpit canopy closed or slid back?; these and many other details are the sort of things to start imagining so that you begin to form a mental picture of what your model will look like when completed. At this stage, also, consider any conversion work or detail changes you may wish to incorporate in the finished model. I deal more fully with these aspects later, but obviously you will need to do all the research for this sort of work in these initial stages. You may need to work out any constructional problems involved in a conversion project well in advance – even before you buy the kit – just to assess the feasibility of the work. You will need to see what scrap parts or accessory purchases are involved.

Similarly, check out at this early stage the intended colour schemes and markings. If you plan to use the markings given in the kit check them for accuracy, as kit makers sometimes make innocent enough errors in their decal sets or colouring instructions so that, for example, the wrong colour is given for cowling markings or an emblem is printed the wrong size on the decal sheet. Finding a picture and details of the real aircraft depicted in the kit is a good way of checking the facts, though most kit reviews, if you can find them, point out any errors of this kind and would save you the trouble. It may be that you plan to discard the markings and colour schemes given in the kit in order to finish the model in a more original way, unique to your collection. In this case even more careful research is needed. If you buy one of the special decal sets available in the hobby stores which provides markings for a specific aircraft, then the decal sheet itself often comes with a colour scheme guide and other reference notes applicable to that particular aircraft. If you decide to come up with some other colour scheme, then you are entirely dependent on your own research efforts. You need to find pictures, colouring details, marking details, and so on. A favourite idea is to find a reliable reference source, such as the Me 109 Profile in the case of our example, and then use the colour illustrations therein as a suitable subject for the model. Your research does not end there, for even this sort of colour artwork can do with cross-checking sometimes, and in addition to this you need to see which markings (in this case, perhaps, German crosses) can be utilized from the kit decal sheet and which may have to be purchased or made up from some other source.

When all these questions are sorted out in your mind you can then start thinking about the actual construction of the model. Meantime, however, just how much time and effort is needed in research for a particular model depends largely on your own accumulated knowledge of the subject, plus the time, space, and money at your disposal. The obscurity (or otherwise) of the aircraft subject you are modelling will also affect the matter. A keen enthusiast, for example, might spend months trying to find out sufficient cockpit or undercarriage details for modelling a specific variant of an aircraft. In the main, however, the bulk of your likely model subjects are well covered in published references and your main problem will be in tracking it down.

Taking into account the personal limitations already mentioned, here are some suggestions for building up your own research and reference library. You may like to follow up all or any of these ideas – just how much you get involved depends really on the time you spend on the hobby and the money you have available for it.

1 Try and take at least one specialist aviation periodical. These magazines are not devoted to modelling (though they may include kit reviews), but they are packed with articles, pictures, drawings, and so on devoted to both current and historical aviation affairs. Among those available are *Air Classics, Air Pictorial, Air Enthusiast, Aircraft Illustrated, Interavia,* and *Aeroplane Monthly.* It may well be that you would not be able to afford more than one, but even if you cannot most public libraries take one or more of these magazines.
Aside from a continuing output of useful reference material, these magazines carry reviews of new books and publications, plus advertisements, and this information alone is often very useful. If you are making the Me 109, for instance, you may recall that a book was published some months earlier on the subject. A quick flip through back issues of one of the specialist magazines will soon reveal any advertisements or reviews indicating the title, author, publisher and price of the book in question. Most of these magazines provide a

yearly index of articles and it is a good idea to keep all issues, space permitting.
2 Try and subscribe to a specialist modelling magazine. Among those available are *Airfix Magazine, Scale Models, Scale Aircraft Modeler, Scale Modeler,* and *Plastik Modell.* These all include articles on specific aircraft conversions with text, drawings, and such things as step-by-step instructions for complicated conversion work. Apart from main articles there are news and reviews of new kits, background articles on real aircraft, and plenty of modelling ideas. Again, try to keep all back issues as in themselves these magazines are a valuable source of reference.
3 Build up a library of basic aircraft reference books in particular on those subjects which interest you – for example, the First or Second World Wars, for example, the First or Second World Wars, Airliners, Fighters, Bombers, etc. The books available run to many thousands with new titles coming out all the time. There are fairly inexpensive works on specific aircraft types, such as Aircraft Profiles, and at the other extreme very

expense encyclopaedias on the subject. A visit to your local public library will give an idea of the sort of books available. Most modellers can afford at least a few books, but even if this is beyond your means, membership of a public library is free, and in any case to be recommended, for no enthusiast could possibly buy (or even want to buy) every book on the subject.

4 Start a scrap-book or some files on aircraft subjects into which you can place any sort of cuttings, written notes taken from books, personal sketches, and so on. For example, even a general interest magazine or newspaper carries the odd article on aircraft – maybe a cut-away drawing of a new jet fighter – especially when the aircraft in question is in the news. Instead of throwing this sort of thing away, cut it out and keep it. If old copies of magazines come your way, peruse them for material worth keeping before discarding them. If space restrictions force you to discard magazines you would prefer to keep, be sure to remove all possible useful articles first. Over the years I have kept a simple filing system in cheap card folders. The sort of classifications you may have (depending very much on your own interests) are 'RAF Fighters, Second World War', 'US Navy Aircraft, Second World War', 'Luftwaffe Bombers, Second World War', 'Civilian Light Aircraft', and so on. When you make a model in any of the categories which interest you, just look out the folder and see what you have available to supplement book and magazine references. My folders contain everything from scale drawings torn from magazines to newspaper cuttings and notes made from books. If your material proliferates just start more folders. For instance you may collect so much material on an aircraft like a Messerschmitt 109 that you start a special 'Me 109' folder additional to a general folder on 'Luftwaffe Fighters'. An alternative to folders is the traditional sort of scrap-book, but once pasted in these, any cuttings are hard to extract or transfer elsewhere. Illustrated here is the author's 'American Helicopters' file which will be used when making up the two Roco helicopter kits shown lower right.

If you have a camera of any sort (even a simple 'Instamatic' type) take it to any airshows, museums, or exhibitions you may visit. Here you get a chance to take any pictures of details you may need. For example, a Spitfire on display may yield you detailed views of the landing wheels, exhaust manifolds, cockpit, and other areas – all as close-up pictures you take yourself. Even aircraft on display, and of no immediate interest to you now, may well turn out to be regarded as a historical relic in ten years time! For instance the F-86 Sabre was once exceedingly common at airshows and the like – now it has almost disappeared and detailed pictures of it at the present time are extremely useful for the aircraft has become a classic and several kits are available. To supplement your own photographs many museums and several firms now sell photographs, postcards, and colour slides, all at modest prices. Keep your pictorial records either in separate boxes or albums, or include them in your filing folders.

5 Typical of the sort of scale plan that can be taken from enthusiasts' magazines and filed for future reference is this fine drawing of the Supermarine S-5. This particular drawing would be most useful for converting the Airfix S-6B kit into the S-5. The drawing is one of a fine series published in the Czechoslovak aviation magazine *Lecktevi + Kosmonautika,* but drawings of this type appear in most enthusiasts' publications.

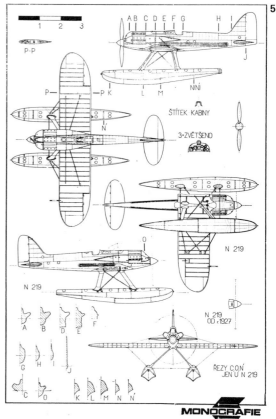

6 Once you have a selection of reference material to hand you are in a good position to get started on the actual modelling work. Here is a typical work bench set-up with scale plan and a selection of pictures and books from the modeller's reference file arrayed in a convenient viewing position. The model here is a Spitfire Mk V.

7–8 If you have a camera try and take it with you on any outings, especially to airfields and museums. These two views of a Cessna T-37A are part of a sequence of 20 or so useful detail shots taken by the author when the aircraft was on display as part of a US Air Force recruiting drive at Eatontown, New Jersey. This type of photograph is invaluable as a modelling reference.

Museums and air displays are themselves a reference source. Actual aircraft and relics are on show, books may be on sale, and archives can be consulted. Above all you can see preserved aircraft of many decades ago which may well have disappeared from service long before you were born. Visit as many airshows and museums as you can. There is a useful reference book by Leslie Hunt, an inveterate worker for aircraft preservation, which logs the location of all known preserved aircraft types. This is called *Veteran and Vintage Aircraft* (Garnstone Press). This by no means exhausts the work you can do in the 'research and reference' field. I have left out TV documentaries, films, and picture libraries, for instance, but all the ideas listed should help you to locate or collect essential information to aid your modelling efforts.

Following page: The Airfix 1:32 scale P-51D Mustang built 'straight from the kit', but with added detail and a Metalskin finish to depict the natural unpainted metal covering of the real aircraft. Model and photo by Gerald Scarborough.

5 : Basic Kit Assembly

Visit any hobby store or plastic kit stockist and you are faced with a bewildering array of model aircraft kits. There is obviously a lot of temptation to make an 'impulse purchase', and the kit manufacturers go all out to persuade you by producing some spectacular kits in lavish boxes. If you are a newcomer to the plastic model aircraft hobby, or maybe a long-time casual modeller who wants to take it more seriously, this is the time to take stock and think about (a) which models you would like to make, (b) which ones you have time to make, and (c) which size and scale you have room to store or display. From this you should arrive at a reasonable compromise which is not too ambitious for either your ability or your spare time.

It is pointless buying a 1 : 32 or 1 : 24 scale model if you have only a single sideboard big enough to display the one model – better perhaps to go to 1 : 100 or 1 : 144 scale and display 12 models in the same area. Similarly if you have never built any plastic kits before do not buy a

1 When you get the kit home, set up your work area, clear the space, open the box, and examine the parts. For a start there may be bits broken or missing – check against the kit instruction sheet or the parts list if such is included. Any missing or damaged parts should be identified at this stage. Most kit manufacturers run a replacement scheme for kit defects. Read the kit instructions, check that you have the right paints and reference material, study your subject and, in fact, do anything except rush into making the model straightaway.

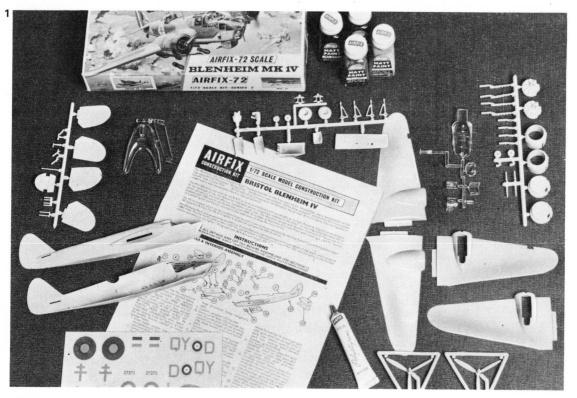

huge complex model which you may never finish – discouraged, maybe, by its bewildering array of parts. Simple models – single place fighters or twin engine types – are the best. All the models illustrated in this section are typical of the sort I would recommend for starters. If you have been reading any of the hobby magazines look for some recent release which may have been reviewed – preferably favourably. That way you will have an idea of a kit's faults or virtues from reading the magazine review. With an older kit you will need to dig around more to find out any errors in the model or improvements you could incorporate – which is where your own reference material comes in. And let me repeat that it's a good idea to know precisely which aircraft you are going to model – right down to colour scheme and serial number – before you begin. Now let us look at the various stages in building up a plastic kit.

Other factors to bear in mind at the assembly stage all involve a degree of forward planning and in most cases they depend on the type of aircraft you are making up. Let me go through them in no particular order, though all are of equal importance.

1. **Will you be using the display stand provided with the kit?** If so make sure the slot provided under the fuselage of the model will actually fit the arm of the display stand. It is frustrating, when the model is completed, having to ruin the paintwork by carving out a larger slot. Recently kit makers have tended to provide a 'blind' slot for the display stand so that those who do not wish to use the stand do not have the trouble of filling it in. Hence if you do want the slot, cut it out *before* kit assembly begins for it may not be possible even to remember where the 'blind' hole falls once the fuselage has been put together. Of course, if you do not wish to use the display stand, anyway, you have the reverse task of filling in the slot where this is present.

2. **Have you checked additional interior requirements for your model?** This is covered again in the next section of the book, but must be borne in mind at assembly stage. For instance the model may be devoid of cockpit floor, or indeed, any kind of cockpit detail. It is usually much more convenient to add all these extra parts *before* the fuselage halves are cemented together. Sometimes, in fact, it is quite impossible to add such details after the fuselage is assembled. Look, too, for snags not covered by the manufacturer's instruction sheet. Some jet plane kits have appeared, for instance, with no kind of bulkhead or fitting inside the

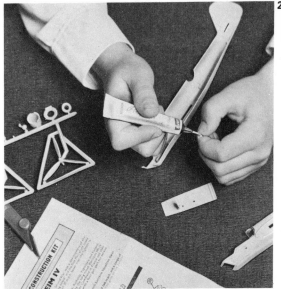

2 In general follow the kit sequence for assembly, having a 'dry run' first to check all parts for fit. Strips of adhesive tape will suffice for holding the main parts together for this. You can use liquid cement (or Mek) for glueing and this is achieved simply by holding the parts snugly together, charging your brush and running it along the join. Surface tension causes the liquid cement to run right into the join. However, I prefer to use ordinary polystyrene cement from a tube for all main joins (fuselage and wing halves, etc.) as this gives a little bit of 'ooze' between the adjacent parts. When the 'ooze' has hardened it can be rubbed down with a fine file or 'wet or dry' paper or fine glasspaper and as often as not there is need for further filling. With liquid cement, on the other hand, the halves may well join together but they may also leave a prominent join line which has to be filled in any case.

3 Here is a badly made model, just to show you what to avoid. On this 1:72 scale Sea Hawk all the parts have been joined up firmly enough but no attempt has been made to eliminate or conceal the join lines, and no painting has been carried out. All the bad joins need to be made good at basic assembly time. The markings on this model are wrongly and crudely applied.

4

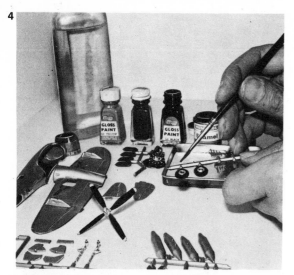

5

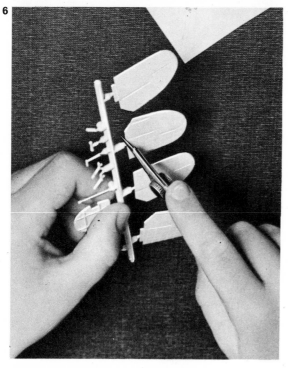

6

engine nacelles, with the result that daylight shows right through the fuselage from end to end and fails to conceal the fact that the model is merely an empty shell with no internals. Some other models have hollow wheel wells, sure enough, but, again, they just reveal an empty hollow engine compartment above them – or daylight showing through the wheel wells. Some action is necessary here, the simplest being the addition of a plastic card bulkhead in any necessary position to obscure the passage of light, and I prefer black plastic card cut quite roughly to fit the inside radius of the fuselage and cemented in place where it will be invisible externally – say at the midpoint of the fuselage. Where wheel wells (or bomb bays, or cargo holds, etc.), need a false roof or floor the circumstances will differ from model to model. Very often there is some convenient inside rib to act

4 In most cases painting starts right at the beginning. It is necessary to paint cockpit interiors (as here), and any other areas which might be inaccessible while the fuselage is still in its component parts. Here wheels, propeller, engine and other components of a P-47D Thunderbolt are being painted.

5 Here's another example of pre-painting. The Hasegawa Fw 190 has its cockpit and engine casing interior painted in the appropriate shade, the latter solely because it is visible through the side cooling gills. On this particular model the engine was painted metallic 'gun metal grey' only as the cowling was cemented firmly in place and the engine was then only visible from the front of the engine nacelle where it is actually almost impossible to see. Had the removable engine cowling feature of this kit been retained it would have been necessary to do a highly detailed paint job on the engine which would have become a major part of the model. Other areas which may need part painting would include wheel wells and bomb bays.

6 Trim parts from the sprues with great care, and file or trim off any rough burrs. Keep small parts on sprues for as long as possible to avoid loss or damage.

opposite above: A good example of kit conversion work. This is the 1:32 scale Airfix P-51D Mustang converted to depict Chuck Hall's Pylon Racer 'Miss R.J.', a much modified ex-USAF machine. Model and photo by Gerald Scarborough.
below: Sopwith Dolphin, a First World War single-seater fighter, which served with the French Air Force. This is a scratch-built model of an aircraft type not available in kit form.

as a support for the new roof or floor, but where nothing exists some small false bulkheads or stringers of suitable height will be necessary. I must stress that this problem occurs more often on very old kits rather than on recent kit offerings; however, even a kit as recent as the Frog HS Buccaneer (produced only a few months before these words were written) was an offender in having a 'hollow' fuselage effect almost exactly as described here, and the work I described is necessary with this particular model.

3. Has your model a tricycle (i.e., nose-wheel) undercarriage? If so you'll need to remember to weight it at the nose in order to ensure that it will actually stand on its nose-wheel rather than tilt back (being tail heavy) and sit on its tail. This requirement is really an extension of point 2. However, failure to remember that nose weighting is required is probably one of the most common of all examples of lack of 'forward planning'. The kit instructions rarely if ever point out the need for weighting the nose, which may well explain why novice modellers often overlook it until too late. Sufficient weight is required packed into the nose to make the model balance at the front, and this is most easily applied before the fuselage halves are joined. Any suitable weight will do – pieces of lead, small nuts and bolts, etc., cemented into place with epoxy or universal type glues. Add the weight in one half of the fuselage so that it protrudes, slightly but not far enough to prevent the other fuselage half from fitting into place. An easier method than glueing is to use modelling clay (like Plasticine) pressed into the inner side of the nose in each fuselage half, and then simply press small metal weights into the clay where they will be held fast. Fishermen's supply shops sell packets of small,

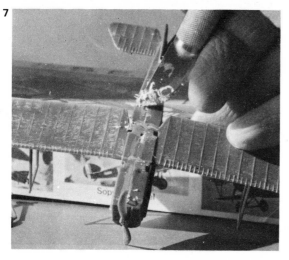

7

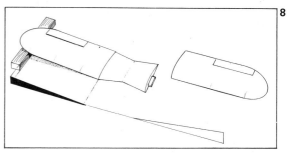

8

7 Elimination of all join lines is the top priority job at basic assembly stage. There is frequently slight distortion in the moulding process so that, say, two halves of a fuselage do not *quite* match up. Generally, there is only a whisker's difference in it, but nonetheless there is not a perfectly flush join. The usual answer here is to line up the top join (along the top of the fuselage) then treat the bottom join to get a flush match. Cement as before, allow to 'ooze' and set hard. Then eliminate the join line by scraping with the blade of a craft knife so that a common smooth join is achieved. The scraping action, rather like the 'adzing' of an old time carpenter, skins off plastic shavings and leaves a smooth join which can then be rubbed down with 'wet and dry' or fine glass-paper. The scraping part of the procedure is here being done on a Revell SE 5A, the bottom fuselage join not matching precisely between the two halves.

8 Many model aircraft are let down by having the incorrect wing dihedral. This is understandable in physical terms. A typical model will have a fuselage with a slot each side for the wings. When you put the tabs on the wing roots into the fuselage slots you will note that there is a lot of play. You would need to guess the correct dihedral angle, hold the wing in place, and then wait for the cement to set hard. In practice this does not happen, so a novice ends up with drooping or horizontal wings when the cement finally sets. To solve the problem more positively, try to obtain a scale drawing of the actual aircraft. From the front elevation draw out an angled template, like the one in this picture. Transfer this to a card cut-out or draw it neatly on paper. Then use the template as a guide to getting the dihedral right. As a card guide it can actually be held under the aircraft while the wings set at the correct angle. One other method is also shown. Where a biplane wing is being assembled, a stripwood block gives support to the wing tips while the wings set. The support is chosen so as to give the correct angle of incidence at the wing tip.

mostly spherical, weights in assorted sizes just right for 1:72 and 1:100 scales. Lead shot can be used in a similar fashion for 1:144 scale or smaller. It is difficult to judge how much weight is needed but a rough idea can be obtained by taping the fuselage halves together (with the nose weights in place) then trying to balance the fuselage on a ruler at the mid-point. If it topples down tail first at every attempt it is a fair bet that a few extra weights will be desirable. As the fuselage is only temporarily taped together it is a simple enough matter to remove the adhesive tape, add a few more items of weight, then try again. When all is satisfactory, the fuselage halves can at last be permanently joined. There are occasional instances where a different approach is needed. The Henschel Hs 219 night-fighter ('Uhu') is a case in point. Here the cockpit is right forward above the nose and there is only a tiny space beneath the cockpit floor where weights can be placed; in this model I compensated by adding weights in the front ends of the engine cowlings out on the wings. But again, these problems must be recognized before you begin, not when construction has got too far advanced to remedy the problem. If all else fails, one way of supporting a model aircraft so that it stands on its nosewheel is to provide a support under the tail or rear fuselage. A trestle made from miniature girdering or an access ladder for the crew is the usual form such a support could take.

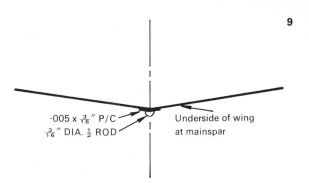

·005 x $\frac{3}{16}$" P/C
$\frac{3}{16}$" DIA. $\frac{1}{2}$ ROD

Underside of wing at mainspar

10

11

12

9 Here is an actual dihedral template for a Mustang. Though drawn mainly for 1:48 and 1:72 scale it can be used for any smaller scale since the dihedral remains constant. Some kits have appeared with a dihedral template included, while other kits, of course, come with one-piece wings, where the dihedral angle is already moulded into the wing and the problem doesn't arise.

10–11 With wings and tail assembled, all joins and blemishes must now be made good. This is done using either Green Stuff or plastic putty, applied smoothly at wing root and tail joins. These are the light areas in this picture. While the putty is setting carry on with other small tasks. The second picture shows the join after rubbing down to give smooth finish.

12 With all the putty set hard (at least overnight) the great clean-up begins. The idea is to eliminate all tell-tale join lines or gaps which cry out that the wings are merely stuck on. Use a file, craft knife, 'wet and dry' paper, or very fine glasspaper. I favour the latter as it is more easily obtainable. As can be seen in this view (where the forward fuselage top is being sanded) the wing and tail roots are rubbed down and there is a smooth transition at each join.

opposite above: This Beaufighter NF Mk I in 1:72 scale combines parts from both Airfix and Frog kits of this aircraft, to give a well detailed replica. Note the effective 'weathered' finish. Model and photo by Alan H. Butler.

below: Bristol Bulldog in 1:48 scale connected to Hucks Starter. This plane was one of the best acrobatic fighters the RAF had. Model by Fred Henderson is constructed from a basic plastic kit. The Hucks Starter is converted from a Ford Model T kit.

13

13 To illustrate some more points here is the underside of a Typhoon in 1:72 scale which is being completed as a prototype. Note that the join line underneath the fuselage has been rubbed down so smoothly that the line is really just a mark on the plastic. Opportunity has been taken to fill the slot for the display stand while the unwanted bomb pylons are removed, as are the gun barrels. The small gaps left by these removals have been filled with plastic putty (light tone) and rubbed down. You can check that join marks have been eliminated just by running a finger over the work. However, an even more foolproof method is to hold the model up to a room light at nearly arm's length and look along the join line at eye level. Any remaining imperfections will throw a shadow; if the join line is completely eliminated it will 'disappear' in the reflected light.

14

14 Some models, especially old ones, are peppered with overscale rivets and there is a large body of opinion among enthusiasts as to the merit (or otherwise) of such surface detailing. The riveting on real aircraft is usually flush and at any distance it becomes virtually invisible though the onlooker is conscious of the riveted surface. Kit makers are, to an extent, making an impression of the real thing, and they include rivet and surface detail, even though it may be overscale. Personally I do not find surface detail objectionable if it is accurately done and kept reasonably fine. Under a coat of paint the surface detail is toned down considerably anyway. However, some models are so overdone with rivets that they are distinctly wrong. The Corsair for instance was flush-riveted and noticeably smooth. So on this particular sample all the rivet detail is sanded off, leaving just the leading panels of the wings as moulded by the makers. The idea of sanding off the rivet detail can be applied to any model.

15 Here is the same Corsair model with rivet and panel detail removed, photographed to show more work in the basic assembly stage. The wings in this case slotted into the belly of the aircraft and there was shrinkage, with a lot of filling needed each side of the wing root. The plastic putty can be seen in white and the filling carried out includes the display stand slot. Filling of this type is necessary on nearly all models for there is frequent shrinkage and mild distortion to be overcome. There are sometimes dimples or die marks visible which also have to be filled in.

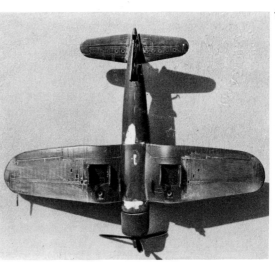

15

4. Are you going to 'motorize' the model? Some small slim-line motors are now available for fitting inside the engine cowling to drive the prop shaft in a realistic fashion. Frog and Airfix are among suppliers of these. Some kits are designed to take the motor with all the necessary supports moulded in (even if the motor is not supplied in the kit). Others can be motorized quite simply and the small electric motors usually come with a leaflet showing the wiring layout and indicating the batteries required for power. In some models the batteries can be fitted into the fuselage, and in others they have to be concealed adjacent to the model, for example in a display base or in some appropriate scenic feature; a favourite is a fuel truck, for the wires to the motor can then be disguised as fuel lines. Motorizing is something of a 'gimmick', though an amusing one. If you do try it, however, you need to think about it before work on the model begins, not after assembly is already under way.

5. Will your model require rigging? If it is a biplane decide your rigging system before you begin. If nylon or terylene is to be used you will need to drill out the anchoring holes *before* assembly begins – and the same, of course, for a monoplane if it is one which is braced with rigging wires. Incidentally, with biplanes it is usual to omit the upper wing until all painting is completed, though the wing itself is tried for fit so that it merely has to be cemented to the top of its support struts. Painting is easy enough even after full assembly, however, on a biplane which is in a single colour like silver dope.

6. Finally if your kit is one of the growing numbers available which offer the choice of several optional parts to allow the model to be completed as one of several possible versions, make quite sure that you identify the appropriate parts for the version which you want to make. Again, once the wrong part is firmly cemented in place it may well be impossible to remove it without ruining the entire model.

An interesting display idea is to complete a large scale model with cut-away sections to show interior detail. This 1:32 scale Hasegawa Hellcat model has been so treated   note cut-outs in engine cowling and cockpit sides. Modifications like this must be made from the initial assembly stages and worked out before building begins.

6: Detailing and Conversion

While the assembly of a plastic kit is basically a very straightforward job, as shown in the last chapter, few really keen modellers are content to make up a model in exactly the same form as it comes in the box. There is always the urge to improve and individualize the kit, even if the changes are minimal – no more, perhaps, than altering the cockpit canopy from the closed to the open position and detailing the cockpit. Conversely it is possible to change a kit in a really big way, maybe even altering it to depict another type of aircraft altogether, or combining parts from several kits or other sources to give a model which is quite unique.

Altering a model from its intended form into another is usually known as a 'conversion', while a change of colour schemes and marking only is often called a 'paint conversion'. Another term sometimes encountered is 'cross-kitting' – when parts from two or more kits are combined to make a new model. Conversion and detail work usually involves cutting, filing, and other physical changes, dependent on the actual project. Personal research, study of any relevant model magazine articles, and perusal of kit reviews in model magazines will show the extent of any conversion work facing the modeller.

In this section there are three different types of work to consider: improving and detailing older kits; models made from conversion kits and accessories; and original conversions.

Improving and Detailing Older Kits

Most modern plastic kits are packed with the sort of detail unknown ten years ago. Many of the latest include optional parts that allow the model to be built in at least two alternative versions, but some have even more parts and combinations included so that as many as six alternatives are possible. Of course, there are model subjects which do not lend themselves

to actual physical variations, but even these usually come with sets of alternative decals so that either one of two or more alternative colour schemes can be selected. To quote just two examples, Jo-han produce some 1:72 scale kits where every subject in the range offers alternative parts and markings. There is a P-47D Thunderbolt, for instance, which features both the 'razorback' fuselage decking and cockpit, and the 'bubble' hood cockpit and low decking. You can make up the model as either version and use one of two alternative decal sets to go with it – or you can use a completely different marking scheme of your own taken from your own reference material. In 1:32 scale there is a fine Harrier 'jump-jet' kit by Revell. This machine has been supplied to both British and American services, a fact reflected by the inclusion of two alternative decal sheets and colour scheme details. The aircraft itself is the same for either service so no actual modelling changes are necessary in this case.

These are typical of modern kit releases, and I should add that the moulding and detail quality is high as is the standard of accuracy, though there are lapses even now in some new kit releases, most often inaccuracies which need correcting. Usually these are of a minor nature. However, there are still scores of old kits available, some of which were released in the 1950s, and most of these are extremely crude by modern standards. Even some kits issued just a few years ago are sparse in detail compared with current offerings. Obviously some old releases have in recent times been replaced by more modern versions of the same model subject, but there remain in circulation a surprisingly large number of old kits which justify collection by the rarity of the model subject.

For example, I have recently acquired Aurora's very old 1:70 scale kit of the Chance-Vought Cutlass US Navy jet fighter of the 1950s. This is a worthwhile addition to a collection of jet fighter types in 1:72 scale, and the kit provides a reasonably good basis for a model. But to bring it to modern standards it needs all the following corrections: rubbing down of grossly over-size rivet detail and panel lines; scribing of new panel lines and control surfaces; removal of the 'solid' cockpit and detailing of same; considerable thinning of wing and tail trailing edges (a frequent task even on very recent kits); and replacement of the under-carriage. The kit depicts the pre-production

version (the first machine, in fact) and for this the decals are correct. If you wanted a produc-tion model, however, several structural changes would be needed, including new nose and cockpit. Not least of the tasks is assembling all the necessary reference material for the work, since the Cutlass is not widely covered in aviation literature.

Here are some examples of the sort of detail changes you may need to make to older kits, or even recent ones with similar deficiencies.

1 Old kits may have undercarriages lacking or the wheelwells may be simply etched outlines on the lower wing surfaces. This Frog Attacker has had the wheelwells cut out with a razor saw and craft knife before the wings were assembled. It is usual to replace over-thick undercarriage doors and flaps with thin plastic card pieces cut to shape. On this particular model the original wheel doors have been retained as they are moulded integral with the oleo legs and replacement would have been awkward. The flaps are, however, being replaced and an original flap has been used to mark out two new ones on the plastic card sheet. Old models with wheelwells awkward to cut out can, nonetheless, have the effect depicted quite well simply by painting in the outline in solid black or using solid black decal sheet, all this being done after the model is fully painted.

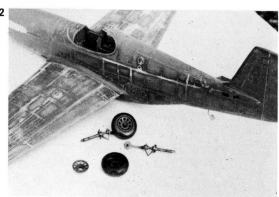

2 Revell 1:32 scale Mustang showing fuselage and wing rivets in process of removal and undercarriage modification. Here, Airfix Lancaster wheels are replacing those in the kit, utilizing the standard hubs and oleo legs. This kit suffers from a slightly inaccurate nose and spinner and poor wheels, while the rivet detail is excessive (Jerry Scutts).

3 A very close view of the underside of a P-51D Mustang in 1:48 scale showing added internal wheel well detail and paint finish with subtle weathering. Note how all join lines have been eliminated – none is visible. Model and photo by A. H. Butler.

4 D/F loops, aerials, pitot tubes, grab handles, small radio antennae, and other minute parts are omitted from most kits, even the most recent ones in many cases. Fine fuse wire or heat-stretched sprue (described on next page) are suitable for most of these. This Me 262, Airfix 1:72 scale, has a D/F loop added, formed by wrapping fuse wire round a knitting needle and nipping off and twisting the end. It is inserted into a tiny hole drilled in position. On this model, also, the tailfin leading edge was modified to give the correct shape. Note the excellent weathered finish (M. Brunon/Paul Camelio).

4

5 Airfix Corsair with modified nose (to depict later mark), excess rivet detail rubbed down, and full complement of small aerials added. The French Navy markings are from a French-made ABT set (C. J. Attard).

5

6 A fine example of an old kit improved and corrected to match modern standards of accuracy and finish. This is the Airfix Westland Whirlwind fighter, originally issued in 1958, given super-detail treatment by A. H. Butler. Note the thinned-down wing trailing edges and added aerials. Changes include extensive alteration to engine nacelles and exhaust, new undercarriage doors and new spinners (A. H. Butler).

6

7 Large scale kits are likely to come with parts for a fully detailed cockpit interior. In smaller scales the cockpit detail is usually either non-existent or at best rudimentary. In some old kits and in several new 1:144 kits there is not even an aperture for the cockpit opening and it will be necessary to cut one. This diagram shows an excellent way of making up a simple but effective cockpit interior. In the case of this particular Gladiator it is necessary to cut a floor, dashboard, and rear bulkhead from plastic card. Control column and foot pedals are made from fuse wire or heat-stretched sprue, depending on scale. The cockpit interior usually has to be made up, painted, and fitted before the fuselage halves are joined, as in the case shown here.

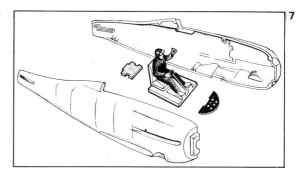

7

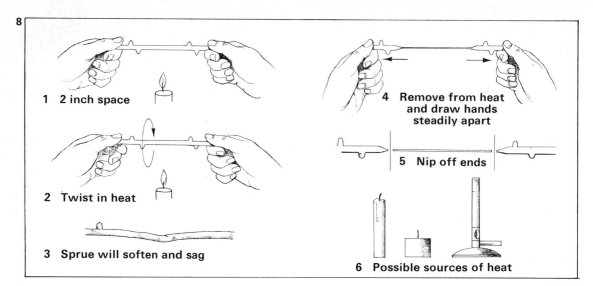

8

1   2 inch space

2   Twist in heat

3   Sprue will soften and sag

4   Remove from heat and draw hands steadily apart

5   Nip off ends

6   Possible sources of heat

8 Already mentioned is the important use of heat-stretched sprue for much of the detail work in plastic kit conversions. The parts of a polystyrene kit come on 'trees' or 'sprues' which are wasted when the kit is made up. Keep the best and longest of these and use them as raw material to make an infinite variety of thin rodding of varying lengths and diameters. Depending on the size achieved, heat-stretched sprue is suitable for rigging wires, exhaust pipes, oleo legs, machine gun barrels, and dozens of other small parts. The precise technique, with some suggested heat sources, is shown here. Sprue can be drawn out to incredibly thin lengths, leaving a filament-like result which is suitable for rigging and aerials. A certain amount of practice is necessary to get good results. Sprue stretching is, perhaps, one of the most useful of all modelling techniques.

9

9 Nearly all biplanes (even from current kits) need wire type rigging to give that final touch of realism. The kit itself gives nothing. The quick way of rigging a model is to use very fine heat-stretched sprue. Prepare several long filament-like lengths preferably from transparent or light colour sprue. Complete the model to painting and decal stage and add the rigging last of all. Measure off the lengths between the relevant anchorage points with a pair of dividers, and use the dividers to measure off a length of the filament. With a pin point, place a tiny blob of white glue at each anchorage point and pop the length of wire into place with tweezers. The tiny blob of white glue will dry transparent. This Pyro/Lifelike Gladiator to 1:48 scale has this type of rigging. Take care to avoid any sagging or kinks (Model Art).

10 An alternative to heat-stretched sprue for rigging work is fine Nylon thread. This has to be anchored. with a tiny knot and cemented. Some large scale kits, like Hasagawa's 1:32 scale biplanes come with pre-drilled holes for Nylon rigging. If you are making a model without holes already in place, drill out anchorage holes before assembly; the rigging is, again, done last of all after painting. This Revell 1:72 scale Boeing P-26 is rigged with Nylon thread (Mihail Moisescu).

Conversion Kits

If you want to make a lot of conversions quickly with the minimum of hard work, then there is now an ever increasing series of specialist kits and accessories designed to be used in conjunction with ordinary kits to make variants or alternatives and thus greatly increase the possible range of models. The German firm of Airmodel pioneered this sort of conversion kit, but there are others available too and conversion kits of some sort can be had now covering certain models in 1:48 and 1:32 scales as well as the many produced for 1:72 scale. The advantage of these conversion kits is that they take the hard work out of the job. So anyone with limited skill who nonetheless has ambitions as a con-

verter will find the kits of value. An example is Airmodel's conversion kit for the Gannet AEW 3. Frog make the original anti-submarine version of the Gannet as a perfectly conventional kit. The Airmodel conversion kit simply provides a new vac-form fuselage and this replaces the original Frog fuselage. The rest of the Frog kit components are used in the normal way. With its very differently shaped fuselage and large belly radome, the Gannet AEW 3 would be quite a difficult conversion job to produce from scratch. Here are illustrated one or two of the models which can be made from conversion kits. One disadvantage of conversion kits is their relatively high price – often more than the kits they are intended to supplement.

11 Air Conversions produce a conversion kit for the Harrier T2 trainer and this is designed to be used with the Frog or Hasegawa kit of the standard single seat version. A new nose and tail is provided, moulded in polystyrene and a new

canopy also comes in the kit. Nose and tail of the kit fuselage are cut off and replaced with the new items from the conversion kit (Richard E. Gardner).

12 This Sabre F-86D conversion kit provides a new vac-form fuselage to replace the F-86F fuselage of the Frog or Hasegawa Sabre. Wings, tail, and other components are used from the original Sabre kit.

13 Rareplanes produced this YP-37A conversion kit which provided a new fuselage and other parts for use in conjunction with the wings, wheels, tail, and canopy of the Airfix P-40 Warhawk/Kittyhawk kit in 1 : 72 scale. This particular item is no longer available.

14 Model Accessories company produce a big series of cut-out printed control panels ideal for detailing model cockpits. Those shown here are to go with Revell 1 : 32 scale kits.

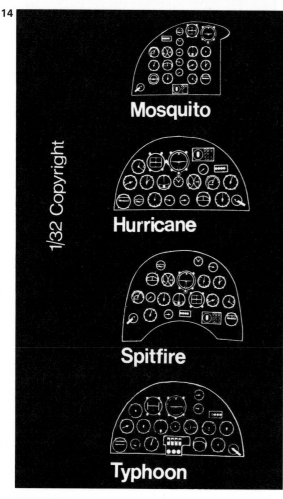

Mosquito

Hurricane

1/32 Copyright

Spitfire

Typhoon

Original Conversions

Long before the days of conversion kits, the only way to make a variation on a standard model was to do all the work yourself. Typically, you might wish to convert a Spitfire IX to a Seafire III. This might involve very little work – new exhaust manifolds, a deck-landing hook, catapult attachment points, and an indication of the wing folding lines – or the folded wings themselves, plus other detail changes. This work you would carry out as you went along. Taking a more complicated example you might wish to make up a Beaufighter kit as a Mk II version with Merlin engines. This would entail removing the Hercules engines provided in a Beaufighter Mk I kit and substituting the Merlin engines, perhaps from a Lancaster kit. This would instantly suggest a third conversion; having a Lancaster kit minus two Merlin engines, the rest of the kit could be used to make an Avro Manchester, the Lancaster's twin engine predecessor. This in turn needs shortened wings, minor fuselage changes, and two new Vulture engines which would need to be scratch-built – maybe carved from balsa wood or made up by cutting down the Merlin engines and reshaping with plastic putty and scrap. The foregoing serves to illustrate that with some careful pre-planning one can keep a good conversion programme going which makes maximum utilization of kits and resources. Conversion possibilities are almost endless and all the various skills and techniques come into play in various degrees. The 'cross-kitting' aspect is well shown in the Beaufighter II example quoted, but there are many other instances. I made a Blackburn Roc Fleet Air Arm turret fighter by adding the turret from a Defiant fighter to a Frog Blackburn Skua. The Defiant, now less its turret, was made up as a target-tug version, so nothing was wasted. Making up an Airfix Anson kit as an unarmed transport or trainer version left the turret available for adding to the Frog Airspeed Oxford. In this instance, also, the nacelles could be switched between the two kits to give a typical engine variation. Some examples of what can be done are shown in the pictures.

15 Messerschmitt Bf 109C is a fine conversion from the Airfix Me 109E in 1 : 32 scale. New cowling, exhausts, propeller, and tail struts are major changes. In 1 : 72 scale Airmodel produce a conversion kit for this variant (Gerald Scarborough).

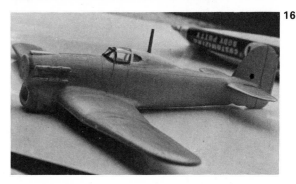

16 A Hawker Typhoon under conversion to its predecessor the Tornado. Note the plugged cannon apertures, the solid cockpit fairing (from half a drop tank), the etched in cockpit doors, the adhesive tape canopy framing, and the engine cowling modifications, including an added air intake from plastic card and plastic putty. In this case the front end of the original Typhoon canopy is used.

17–20 This sequence of pictures shows the stages in converting the Frog DH Hornet from the RAF fighter version to the Fleet Air Arm night fighter version (NF 21). The white and light coloured areas are plastic putty, plastic card, or plastic scrap. This model has been given folding wings, utilizing a simple plastic card dummy hinge. Note extended tailplane and deck-landing hook. Completed model has markings made up from various spare decals, and reproduces well the semi-gloss finish of 1950s naval aircraft (Keith Palmer).

21 A classic example of an advanced conversion superbly carried out. The YB-17A, the original version of the Flying Fortress is converted from the Airfix B-17G. A new rear fuselage and tailfin is fitted, carved from wood and covered with Metalskin so that it is not obviously wood. There are extensive detail changes elsewhere, especially to the nose. With an impeccable standard of finish the model is a wonderful showpiece conversion (Gordon Stevens).

22 A further example of a 'cross kitting' conversion This is a Rareplanes Seversky P-35 (now out of production) fitted with a cowling and propeller from an Airfix Flying Fortress to depict a non-standard civilian racer version of the P-35. The pilot figure in characteristic garb greatly enhances the model and is converted from a model soldier (Gordon Stevens).

21

22

23 One final trick when converting is the occasional need for a new moulded canopy or radomes, drop tanks, and similar. This can be done with clear acetate sheet in the case of cockpit canopies, or thick plastic card. The drawing sequence shows how it's done. With careful planning – and there are plenty of conversions to choose from – you can avoid this sort of chore almost all the time. It is time consuming, messy, and often takes several attempts to get a satisfactory result

23
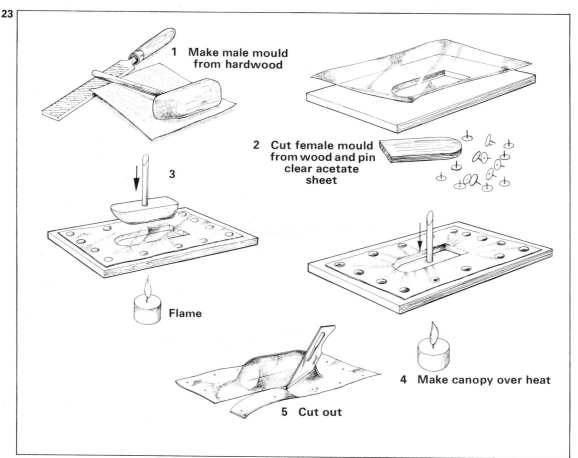

1 Make male mould from hardwood

2 Cut female mould from wood and pin clear acetate sheet

3

Flame

4 Make canopy over heat

5 Cut out

7: Painting and Finishing

Paints

Like kit building and converting, the painting of model aircraft need not be an enormously expensive or complicated business, but conversely you can spend a small fortune on paint, equipment, and materials if you happen to have the money available. In recent years the kit and accessory manufacturers have concentrated extensively on the paint side of the hobby so that model painting today does not have too many pitfalls for the unwary. Virtually any shade required for aircraft modelling is available in the paint ranges currently being produced, though admittedly there is no guarantee that your local hobby store will have them in stock. Some years ago the situation was somewhat different; then there was a selection of 'pretty' colours available plus some of the more common camouflage colours. The aircraft modeller then had to work out actual shades for himself, if necessary carrying out elaborate mixing (and time-consuming experimentation) to arrive at authentic shades for models. The result was a good deal of approximation and guesswork, dependent largely on the skill and colour sense of the modeller.

The British paint firm of Humbrol changed all that; in 1967 they started introducing an 'Authentic Colours' series which set out to provide tinlets of carefully matched shades corresponding to the actual original colours used by the world's major air forces. Happily the series prospered; today there is a huge range available and it is quite rare for the average modeller to need to mix some special shade for himself – though the situation can and does arise if you choose an unusual model subject.

Because the Humbrol paint series is the biggest and most important range available I have listed here all the most important sets of specific interest to the aircraft modeller. The reference numbers given (e.g. HB1) are the maker's catalogue numbers and are carried on the tins and the hobby store dispenser unit from which the paints are sold:

Kit 1 Royal Air Force (European)
HB1 Dark Green; HB2 Dark Earth; HB3 Ocean Grey; HB4 Duck Egg Blue; HB5 Sky Type S; HB6 Sea Grey Medium.

Kit 2 Luftwaffe
HG1 Schwarzgrun 70 (Black Green); HG2 Dunkelgrun 71 (Dark Green); HG3 Hellgrau 76 (Light Grey); HG4 Dunkelgrau 74 (Dark Grey); HG5 Hellblau 65 (Light Blue); HG6 R.L.M. Grau 02 (R.L.M. Grey).

Kit 3 USAF
HU1 Medium Green 42; HU2 Olive Drab 41; HU3 Neutral Grey 43; HU4 Non Specular Sea Blue; HU5 Intermediate Blue; HU6 Light Grey.

1 Model paints are usually displayed at your hobby store in a dispenser. This is Humbrol's version for their 'Authentic Colours' range described in the text. Each colour is marked with a patch and its description and catalogue number.

Kit 4 Fleet Air Arm

HB7 Extra Dark Sea Grey; HB8 Dark Slate Grey; HB5 Sky Type S; HB9 Sea Blue Gloss; HB10 Night Black; HB11 Underside White.

Kit 5 Royal Air Force (Overseas)

HB2 Dark Earth; HB12 Mid Stone; HB13 Azure Blue; HB10 Night Black; HB11 Underside White; HB14 Airframe Silver.

Kit 6 French Air Force

HF1 Kaki (Khaki); HF2 Vert (Green); HF3 Terre Foncée (Dark Earth); HF4 Gris Bleu Clair (Light Blue Grey); HF5 Gris Bleu Fonce (Dark Blue Grey); HF6 Chocolat (Chocolate).

Kit 7 Italian Air Force

HI1 Mottle Green; HI2 Upper Green; HI3 Overall Green; HI4 Sand; HI5 Grey; HI6 Insignia White.

Kit 8 Japanese Air Force

HJ1 Green N1; HJ2 Grey A/N2; HJ3 Green A3; HJ4 Mauve N9; HJ5 Brown N17; HJ6 Silver A6.

Kit 9 USAF (Vietnam)

HU7 Green 34079; HU8 Green 34102; HU9 Tan 30219; HU10 Grey 36622; HU11 Airframe White; HU12 Night Black.

Kit 12 World War 1 Aircraft

HB15 R.F.C. Green; HB16 Clear Doped Linen; HG7 German Pale Yellow; HG8 German Green; HG9 German Purple; HG10 German Light Blue.

Kit 13 NATO Aircraft

HX1 Dark Green; HX2 Dark Sea Grey; HX3 P.R.U. Blue; HX4 Sea Grey Medium; HX5 Light Aircraft Grey; HX6 Extra Dark Sea Grey.

Kit 14 Russian Aircraft

HT1 Topside Green; HT2 Underside Blue; HT3 Surface Grey; HT4 Subframe Grey; HT5 Marker Red; HT6 Insignia Yellow.

Kit 16 Cockpit Colours

HG6 R.L.M. Grau 02 (R.L.M. Grey); HD1 Aircraft Grey-Green; HD2 Bright Green; HD3 Night Blue; HD4 Zinc Chromate Primer; HD5 Interior Green Ana 611.

The paints are sold in boxed sets as listed – very useful if you are a beginner – but the tinlets (which are $\frac{1}{2}$ ounce size) can be purchased singly as well. There are additional sets in this range covering military and scenic subjects.

There are, of course, many other paint ranges available. Very widely sold, especially in the United States, Canada, and Britain, are the Testor and Pactra paints, made in USA and Canada. Quite a few of the camouflage shades offered by Humbrol are closely matched by Testor and Pactra with similar or identical names. Another big range, sold mostly in Europe, is the French-made Modelcolor series, almost as diverse as Humbrol's range, and again produced in specific 'authentic' shades. In Britain (and also available elsewhere) is the useful Airfix paint range which, again, includes the more common camouflage shades, plus other colours. The camouflage shades match Humbrol's quite closely though the selection is much smaller. I mention these various brand names simply because hobby stores do not necessarily stock more than one of them so you may need to buy substitutes. Humbrol produce a very useful 'Authentic Camouflage Colours' free leaflet complete with colour patches. If you can get one of these it makes a handy reference for you can use it to match shades from other brands if you need to.

All the brands so far mentioned have an extensive range of 'pretty' colours available for general model and hobby work – so there are numerous shades of reds, blues, yellows, greens, and so on. Mostly these are in gloss but several of the more common colours are also produced in matt. For airliners and other non-military aircraft models these colours come into their own, of course.

Humbrol produce yet another range of paints valuable to aircraft modellers – the Railway Enamels, intended for model trains. These colours are all semi-matt, actually just right for a gloss or polished finish on a modern aircraft. The shades are all railway colours, but many of them match aircraft or Service shades, or can be mixed to match.

All the paints so far described are in the 'pocket money' price range. Most paint makers produce a listing or even a leaflet of colour patches. Collect any such literature and keep it with your reference material.

In addition to what might be called the 'ordinary' paints, there are numerous smaller more specialized brands. Of these Floquil is a well-known and respected name. The Floquil paints are thin and cover well. However, a major word of warning is needed here: Floquil paint is, as a rule, not suitable for direct application to bare plastic as used in kits. It is lacquer-based and eats into the surface of some plastics, so Floquil produce a special 'barrier' varnish which should be applied to the plastic model before the painting begins. If in doubt, try it on a piece of scrap plastic first.

Most paint ranges sold today are suitable for application to plastic and the term 'plastic paint' or 'plastic enamel' is often used to describe them. Avoid using any paint which is cellulose-based. This sort of paint is intended for non-plastic models. Used on plastic it will simply attack the surface, causing buckling or other ruinous effects.

A recent development is the appearance of water-soluble paints which can be applied to plastic and other surfaces – brushes can, of course, be washed in water after using these. The best known range is Polly S, made by the Floquil firm. Some experienced modellers use gouache or acrylic paints (available in art shops) but these are expensive and are beyond the needs of the average modeller.

To round off this survey of the types of paint available, there is the need to mention matt and gloss clear varnish, and Humbrol's Flatting Agent. The clear varnishes are self-explanatory (though I should mention that they usually require extra thorough stirring – up to 5 minutes – to ensure that they set hard after application). The flatting agent, made by Humbrol, comes in a tube. A portion of flatting agent is added into the basic colour in use, and, again after thorough mixing, the colour will dry matt. This very useful material means that virtually any gloss colour can be toned down to matt finish if required. Using less flatting will, of course, make the paint less matt and more glossy. Proportions for mixing are given on the tube. Too much flatting agent incidentally, will 'kill' the paint completely and it will dry out powdery and white. Last of all on the material side comes white spirit for brush cleaning and thinners for paint mixing. The main paint makers include these materials in their ranges.

It is worthwhile taking care of paints and varnishes. Modern plastic enamels can be spread very thinly, and dry quickly, free of brush-marks if properly applied. They need thorough stirring – pieces of scrap plastic sprue are suitable for this – and tinlet lids (or screw tops if appropriate) should be firmly affixed as soon as the paint is finished with. Leaving tins open for any length of time – or with loose lids – will allow a skin to form on the paint. After a period the paint may start to go thick and lumpy, or the pigment may settle hard at the bottom of the tinlet. A little thinners can often rejuvenate old paint, but it is better still to discard the tin

and get a replacement. Matt and gloss clear varnish goes 'off' even sooner, and sometimes becomes discoloured. Replace it frequently. If you have paint tins stored unused for any period it is a good idea to turn them upside down for a week, then back the other way the next week, etc, to prevent the paint from settling. To keep track with replacement needs, one idea is to mark the date of purchase on the tinlets.

Brushes

The importance of brushes tends to be overlooked by beginners who are often content with any old cheap brush of dubious origin. These sorts of brushes, sold in many chain stores and small shops, are intended for children's painting books rather than the rigours of model painting and they quickly lose their shape AND their hairs – the hairs come off and stick to the painted surface of your model! For successful painting it is more economical in the long run to buy a few top quality brushes which will last rather than a succession of cheap hair-shedding

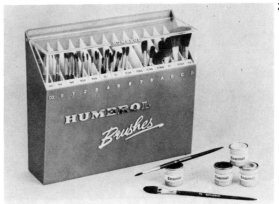

2

2 This hobby store brush dispenser shows in convenient form a typical series of brushes, ranged and numbered in size from left to right. The brushes graded A–D are heavy duty type, too big for small scale aircraft work. In the foreground is a chisel-edged brush, very useful for aircraft painting. Some ½-ounce tinlets are also shown.

examples. Art shops usually have a good selection at varied prices – the quality matching the price – and it is as well to buy the best you can afford. These are usually camel or sable hair and sizes run from 000 to 00, then 0, then 1 upwards. Sizes 00 or 0, then 1 up to 5 (not necessarily all) make a good selection likely to cover all general painting needs. In addition to these you need at least one chisel-edged flat brush which is particularly useful for certain types of painting, notably 'feathering' edges at the demarcation of two differing colours. It is also used for painting large areas. For varnishing work it is as well to keep a separate brush and it is a good idea to relegate any old brush for this purpose. And, finally, very important, is a 'stippler' brush – an old brush with the bristles cut off to leave only a stump 2–3 mm deep. This is for use in mottling or similar work where a random or light application is needed. Brushes should be kept scrupulously clean at all times. Do not leave them standing, either in paint or out of it when they have once been used.

White spirit or brush cleaner in a shallow tin or jar suffices for getting off the paint. Work the spirit out on a piece of thick card or wood, and wash out the paint-free brush in slightly soapy water. Then dry off with tissues or cloth, restore the flat or pointed shape with the fingers, and return all brushes to a safe receptable – maybe the box in which you keep your paints or else in a jar where they can be kept free from crushing, or distortion.

Brush Painting

In theory there is nothing more than common sense and a calm approach needed for painting model aircraft, but a lot of well-made models get spoiled at this stage either by slapdash

3 It is better to choose simple colour schemes rather than complicated multi-colour schemes if your painting skill is limited or if you are a beginner. Nichimo's 1:48 scale A6M5C Zero 52 made by J. Groeneveld shows that plain single colour upper and lower surfaces are nonetheless effective for being simpler to apply (J. Groeneveld).

brushwork or inadequate preparation.

The early stages of painting a model are closely linked to your research and reference work and, indeed, you should have decided on colour scheme and markings before you began the model – or at least by the early construction stages. As indicated earlier in the book, a good deal of painting is carried out as construction

proceeds. Interiors, wheels, oleo legs, propeller, engines, and so on are all either inaccessible or awkward to reach after the model is assembled, so all that can be conveniently painted at the early stages should be dealt with. It is easy to paint small items while they are on the kit sprue and they can be touched up later if necessary after affixing to the model.

On the assumption that the model is basically complete – or at least ready for main painting – make a final check, in particular looking for joins where the actual join line has still not been eliminated. It is very common to find that the underside of the fuselage and wing roots are at fault here. Many otherwise excellent models which I've examined have looked perfect from the top but still show prominent join lines through the paint when inspected from underneath. The constant handling which the model has received, plus the inherent greasy film it carries from the mould, means that washing and drying to remove these substances are the first tasks. Clean out all crevices and interior surfaces with a large soft brush. Then gently wash the airframe using a scrap of sponge and a saucer of water with one or two drops of soap solution added (i.e., liquid detergent). With a fairly 'dry' wash, the model will soon dry out.

On all my aircraft models I always apply an undercoat, though there are exceptions to this general rule, which I will deal with later. For aircraft which are either overall silver or in light colours, use matt white. For camouflage colours and dark colour schemes I favour a matt grey, such as No. 27 in the standard colours range made by Humbrol. Aside from giving a good surface for the top coat, these undercoats are valuable in other ways. For a start they 'seal' any body putty or similar filler for these materials are often slightly porous and would show through a directly applied top coat. Secondly any model defects previously unnoticed will most certainly show through the undercoat. Some typical points which might show up include the following: (1) Imperfect or incomplete panel detail – e.g. smoothing out a join line might well mean that an engraved panel line is rubbed down; the undercoat will draw attention to this and remind you to score back the panel line. (2) Small gaps in join lines will show – e.g. though you may have cemented upper and lower wing halves together, the undercoat may well reveal a tiny crack at some point or other along the edges where the cement was applied too sparsely. (3) Hairline cracks have been known to appear in thinner plastic parts like tailplanes; these may not be immediately obvious on unpainted plastic but they certainly show up through a thin matt white or grey undercoat.

Any defects which are revealed on the above lines should, of course, be remedied and the affected area can be given another undercoat. At the undercoat stage you can still do any necessary filing, sanding, or filling, whereas any need to do this after the topcoat stage will either mar the finish, make much more repainting necessary, and could, in general, undo the work of many hours.

The types of paint most suitable for application to model aircraft have been dealt with already. Though these are mostly thought of as being for use with plastic models, they are equally applicable to wooden models, provided that the surface is suitably prepared first. Some miscellaneous hints on paint should be considered first. To start with the various camouflage colours supplied ready mixed depict what might be called 'factory fresh' paint. Articles in enthusiasts' magazines are often very dogmatic about paint shades as though, for instance, every pot of a certain standard colour contained precisely the same shade. In actual fact paint for aircraft is usually made to contract, often by several companies. Though they would work to precise specifications, shades, say of dark green, might vary in intensity (but not by much) between makers. Storage, temperature, and the materials and mixes used could all affect the shade – even the primer finish on the aircraft could affect it. Add to this the effects of weathering on the paint after application and it is apparent that in a batch of similar aircraft there could be latitude in shade. The weathering in particular has a noticeable effect. This can be seen more strikingly on brightly coloured commercial airlines than on camouflaged warplanes. In particular, next time you pass an airport, note how faded and patchy any red areas can become on civil aircraft.

I deal with weathering as such later, but meantime while engaged in the basic painting work you may wish to tone down the colours a little to take 'aging' into account. A touch of white or yellow lightens darker colours – one or two drops is usually all that is required. For light colours a touch of black or grey tones them down in a subtle way. The study of plenty of aircraft pictures – or better still real aircraft is commended to assist in understanding this problem. Some paints pose special problems. Silver in particular can be awkward. 'Matt' and 'Gloss' silvers are available – though they never seem to me to be all that different. For fabric finishes, as on pre-war military aircraft, matt silvers look

fine. White undercoating is essential unless the plastic of the model is silver in colour, in which case I have found that an undercoat can be dispensed with. There is a silver shade in the Humbrol Railway Enamels series which I find very good to depict metal silver coloured panels. On pre-war period RAF biplanes, for example, where the engine cowling was metal clad and the remaining surfaces were fabric. I've used the Railway Enamels silver for the metal areas and matt silver for the fabric areas. The contrast really is noticeable. I've also used the Railway Enamels silver for painting 'natural metal' aircraft and the effect is quite reasonable. At this point, though, let me say there are more realistic ways of depicting natural metal and I deal with these later. Many modellers will be happy to stay with silver paint, however, and if you are depicting a natural metal finish with silver paint only, use at least two different brands of silver and pick out some of the panels in the second shade to get the effect of multi-texture metalling which is almost invariably seen on unpainted metal-clad aircraft. On the subject of silver finishes, there are, of course, instances of silver-painted aircraft. Again the silver shade varies from a bright tone to a greyish-silver. For instance, there was a 'High Speed Silver' applied to post-war RAF jet fighters which was quite dull. A little grey mixed with the silver depicts this variation quite well. Silver paints, incidentally, age even sooner than other paints.

One further idea worth trying and which works very well is to use the natural plastic, where this is silver, to depict a weathered natural metal finish. This cannot be done where

4

4 Tamiya's 1 : 100 scale **SAAB Viggen** is here shown in natural metal finish, achieved by buffing up the silver plastic in which the model is moulded. This technique is effective in any scale if the silver plastic is of a suitable shade and quality.

the silver plastic is streaky, but on more recent kits the plastic is often of uniform silver throughout. After assembly the plastic is simply buffed up and polished, and paint is used only for detail parts, anti-dazzle panels, and so on. Flawless assembly work, with no cement marks on the model surface, is essential.

Reds, yellows, and some greens are fairly transparent and these must have an undercoat. Reds, in particular, usually need a second coat as well.

Just like water-colours in a paintbox, most model paints can be mixed together to give other shades. To be on the safe side I always restrict this mixing to paints of the same brand. A mixing palette of some kind is desirable. An up-turned tin lid or half a plastic egg box makes a suitable palette. The paint should be stirred in its tin first – very thoroughly – and then a suitable portion for the job in hand should be put

into the palette. While one can pour out a little paint just by tilting the tin, some sort of ladle makes the task cleaner. An old salt or mustard spoon is ideal if you can find one, this being a true miniature ladle where proportions can be very accurately measured. This sort of measure really comes into its own, where an unusual shade is required. A flat ice lolly stick offers another way of getting a small measure of paint. Dip it into the paint tin and sufficient paint adheres to run a small quantity off on to your mixing tray. Kit instructions or a magazine article may say something like 'To obtain this shade mix two parts dark green to one part yellow and one part red'. With a small ladle this becomes a very quick precise operation. When toning down a colour in the manner previously suggested, the paint should be put into the palette first, then the few drops of additional colour added and mixed in. Avoid pure black

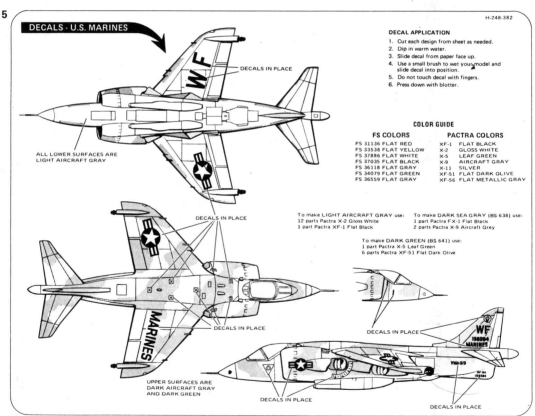

5 Recent top quality kits contain excellent painting guides which are usually very accurate – though it is still wise to cross-check from other reference sources. This is part of the colour scheme guide from Revell's fine 1 : 32 scale Harrier kit. It will be noted that this particular sheet gives precise instructions for mixing the correct shades for the colours from Pactra paints (Revell (GB) Ltd.).

above: The famous P-51D Mustang is produced in kit form in virtually every scale. This is the 1:48 scale version by Monogram, here made up with added detail and with a superb paint finish. The name and squadron markings are hand painted. Model and photo by Alan H. Butler.

below: North American T-28 trainer which served as a US Navy training plane. This is made from a 1:48 scale Monogram kit. Note the detailed cockpit interior.

incidentally, even on an all-black aircraft. A touch of white – more than a touch for 'rubber' – turns the colour to very dark grey in effect and this looks more like black than true black itself. Obviously there are many occasions when paint can be applied after stirring directly from the tin with no prior need for decanting on to a palette.

The actual technique of brush painting demands nothing more than intelligent use of the materials. The rules, in fact, are much the same as for domestic paint jobs like painting a door. For simplicity I have enumerated these in order.

1. Where possible lightly mark out any demarcation lines with a soft pencil over the matt undercoat. For example, the line along the fuselage where upper and lower colours meet, or the divisions of a multi-colour upper surface scheme, e.g., two tone camouflage or the horizontal divisions of a light civil aircraft's colours. Obviously the information for this sort of work is taken from your reference material.

2. Check that you have all the colours needed to hand, and that the paint is in good condition. Obvious as this may seem, it is easily overlooked. I have sat down to paint a model, reached the third colour and opened the tin only to find the paint dried up inside. It may be some days even before you can get a replacement. Check that your colours are matt and semi-matt as required. Again in the past I have come across instances where what was thought to be a tin of matt paint turned out to be gloss and quite unsuitable for the job in hand. If in doubt on any point, this is the time to paint a test piece on scrap plastic before risking your chance on the model itself.

3. Modern model paints like Humbrol and Testor are invariably thin and smooth – at least when new – and they spread easily and evenly. Depending on brand and type the drying time (to 'touch dry', if not fully dry) is anything from 5 minutes to one hour, with the tendency towards the shorter period now. If the paint is thin and free-running then visible brush marks will be avoided. Thick paint can be reduced to a more workable consistency by the discreet addition of thinners and very vigorous and thorough stirring. If the paint is not only thick but full of bits of skin and lumps, and if there is a lot of caking, then it is sounder to discard the tin and buy a replacement.

4. Do not overload the brush. Just the lower half of the bristles should be dipped into the paint. If paint runs freely off the brush as you lift it from the paint then you are picking up too much paint. Hold the brush at its metal part, close up to the bristles – this gives maximum control over the end. The brush will pivot about your fingers and it can be seen that holding the handle half way up will allow the bristles to be deflected too easily and the end of the brush to waver around over a large arc.

5. Apply the paint in short even strokes – chordwise across a wing for instance. It is good practice to keep the bristles actually on the model surface while all the paint in one loading of the brush is worked out. Lifting the brush and stabbing it back again can lead to noticeable brush marks and uneven coverage. The alternative to a back and forth action without lifting the brush is to brush in one direction only. A chisel-ended brush is convenient for covering large areas quickly. Be sure not to allow paint to build up against surface detail on the model; this is only too easy, especially if your paint is too thick or your brush is overloaded. Runs or 'curtains' are also the result of too liberal application of paint. Be specially careful at edges of wings, etc. A good way with wing leading edges is to run the side of the brush along them to get a neat line of paint.

6. Often you only need one application of a paint coat, but where a second is found necessary ensure that no attempt is made to cover the first coat for at least 12 hours. Premature application of a second coat could well lead to the first one lifting, or stripping off in parts, with predictably devastating results. If this does happen you have no alternative but to leave the whole lot to set hard then rub down the whole surface with 'wet and dry' paper before starting all over again. It is generally more satisfactory to make careful application of two or three thin coats than try to cut corners with one thick sloppy coat.

7. Similarly do not attempt to apply second colours before the first coat is dry. Obviously any attempt to do so can lead to colours running into each other with disastrous results. In this connection an aircraft model with a multi-colour camouflage scheme offers two alternative approaches. Take a Hurricane with a dark earth and dark green colour scheme. The 'correct' way of painting this to get an even paint coverage is to paint the dark earth areas first, then when these are dry paint in the dark green so that they butt. With modern thin matt paints, however, it is possible to paint the model's upper surfaces overall in dark earth, then painting the dark green areas over the dark earth. This is certainly easier than painting each area separately.

8. On many camouflaged aircraft the colours are 'feathered' into each other with a soft edge where the paint is applied by spray on the real aircraft.

'Feathered' edges are achieved by using either a chisel-edged or trimmed down 'stippling' brush and moving this along the demarcation line with a gentle jiggling (up and down) motion. One of the pictures makes this clear. Two brushes are needed for this; apply the area of darker colour over the lighter colour up to the actual demarcation line. Then with the second 'stippling' brush produce the 'feathered' edge.

9. Mottling of a second colour over a lighter colour is another variation of this. It is commonly seen on Second World War German and Italian aircraft where, say, dark green can be mottled over sand colour. Here the technique is to paint the main base colour. When this is dry take your cut-down 'stippling' brush and use this almost dry to apply a light mottle, again by a gentle jiggling (up and down) motion. To get a 'dry' brush, dip just the bristle end of your 'stippling' brush into the surface of the paint, then work it out on a piece of scrap plastic or plastic card to ensure that the brush really is 'dry'. Following your reference material closely, start at a high point, such as the fuselage centre-line and begin to apply the mottle with a gentle stabbing action of the brush. Work out from the centre-line as required. Some aircraft with mottle schemes, especially Luftwaffe types, had the pattern only on the upper fuselage, fading away to nothing on the sides. Other aircraft would be mottled all over the upper surfaces, rather like a spotted dog. As a general rule apply mottle camouflage very gently and sparingly to start with, gradually working up to the intensity shown in the reference drawings for any given model. It is easy enough to keep adding mottle but difficult to remove too much without starting all over again.

As an alternative to a cut-down 'stippling' brush some modellers use a very small piece of bath sponge for mottle application, used in the same general way as the brush. Personally, however, I find the brush method more controllable.

10. Some aircraft had a variation on a mottle finish in the way of a ripple or wave pattern camouflage. Here, instead of feathered patches,

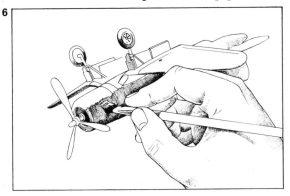

6 Using a chisel-edged brush to paint in the 'feathered' demarcation line between upper and lower surface colours on a wartime US Navy aircraft. This picture also shows the correct way to hold the brush – close up on the metal end.

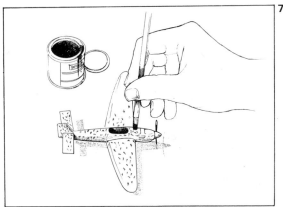

7 'Stippling' being done with a cut-down paintbrush to achieve a mottle finish as described in the text.

8 Revell's 1:32 scale model of the Focke Wulfe FW 190D finished in splinter pattern camouflage with the characteristic mottle finish fuselage sides. The mottle effect has been achieved by 'stippling' with a cut-down brush. Note the spiral marking on the spinner, a tricky piece of hand painting which needs practice to perfect (Les Whitehouse).

9 Another example of a mottle finish applied by 'stippling' with a cut-down brush. For this extremely light type of mottle a very dry brush is essential. This is Hasegawa's 1:32 scale Me 262A made straight from the kit (Gerald Scarborough).

the camouflage was applied like small squiggles all over the base colour. For this sort of scheme there is no real alternative to brush painting. Here a small No. 'o' brush would be used and the squiggles need application by hand.

11. Paint in detail items last of all. This might include picking out exhaust manifolds, collector rings, and bare metal jet pipes, plus touching up of previously painted small parts such as propeller blades.

12. Cockpit canopies and other transparencies are best left to last, except where the mode of construction necessitates, say, a turret being assembled integral with the fuselage. Any such transparencies can be protected from damage or scratching while assembly proceeds, simply by covering them over with strips of clear adhesive tape. On more recent kits I find that canopies and turrets are usually very neatly

engraved with framing lines. These are mostly good enough to permit freehand painting of the framing using a No. 'oo' brush. The fine engraved lines act as a good guide. Any spots of trouble where paint might smudge on to the transparency can be taken care of with the point of a wooden cocktail stick; pick off any smudges or plops. Avoid using thinners to clean up the smudges from transparencies – thinners can mark clear plastic.

The alternative to this is to use fine strips cut from transparent parcel tape. The drawings show how this is done; essentially the tape is put on a cutting surface, painted to match the required colour scheme, then cut into strips for use as required to make up the framing.

10 Some aircraft had a camouflage finish with irregular shaped patches rather than mottle. This sort of pattern must be applied by brush using a small (No. 'O' or 'OO') brush and following references carefully. This is Revell's Kawasaki Toryu in 1:72 scale in the markings and finish as provided in the kit. The canopy framing is also hand painted following the etched lines on the transparencies.

11 One of the most difficult of all aircraft colour schemes to reproduce convincingly is the German 'lozenge' pattern of the First World War. It can only be hand painted, though it is possible to produce a paper template to assist in positioning. On this model it has been achieved very well, as has the characteristic streaky demarcation on the fuselage sides, obtained by 'dry brushing'. Model is the Airfix 1:72 scale Hannover (Airfix Products Ltd.).

12 These diagrams show the method of cutting and affixing thin adhesive tape to depict canopy framing. Paint the tape to match the aircraft colour before cutting. Peel the strips of tape off the cutting surface with tweezers (Bryan Fosten).

10

11

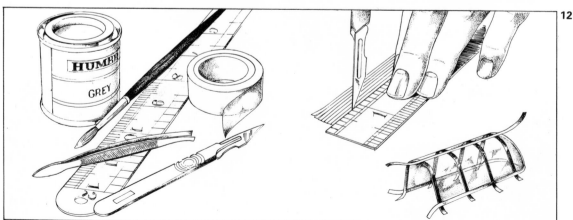

12

13 This is the sort of realistic finish which can be achieved by skilful air-brushing. It is specially effective in camouflage schemes which feather into each other as on this RAF Buccaneer S2. Note however, that brush painting is still required for the canopy framing, tyres, oleos, and intake lips. Reproduced larger than life, this is Tamiya's 1:100 scale model (Tamiya Mokei Ltd.).

below: Short Scylla, of which only two were made for Imperial Airways. This is a fine example of a scratch-built model in plastic card. It is 1:72 scale and made by Tony Woollett.

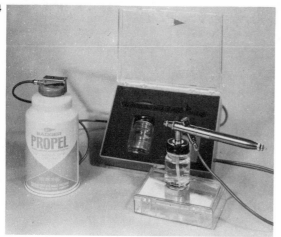

14 This is one of the least expensive airbrush outfits, the Badger 400 which costs around £5 (about $12). The paint in this case is carried in a small jar and a second jar is provided in the set for quick changes. The propellant 'bomb' is on the left and in this case has only a simple on/off switch. This machine cannot achieve such fine line work as the more expensive models, but it is perfectly adequate for general work, such as applying a typical multi-colour camouflage scheme (Morris and Ingram).

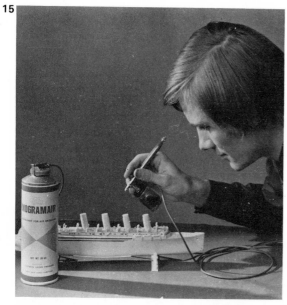

15 This picture shows well the way of holding an airbrush, though the subject shown here being undercoated is a ship. The brush is held rather like a fountain pen, and the forefinger works the button to control the size of the nozzle. As shown here the nozzle is fully open and the brush is about the right distance from the subject for general painting, e.g. for a basic overall colour. For finer work the button is pushed in (there is a very small range) to produce a 'tighter' spray and the nozzle is then held much closer to the subject (Morris and Ingram).

Airbrushing

With care, model aircraft to any scale can be very neatly finished by brush painting only. Most modellers are satisfied to stick to brushes and aircraft in the smaller scales can be finished quite satisfactorily with careful work. Most full-size aircraft, however, are painted wholly, or in part, with a spray gun. This leads to such oft-mentioned phenomena as 'feathering' at the demarcation line – a soft edge between two adjacent colours caused by the spray effect when the colours are applied. Though this can be simulated in miniature with careful brushwork, there is no denying that a scaled down paint spray can do the job even more realistically. The very thing is available (and has been for years) – the airbrush. This, as its name implies, is a tool for applying paint using air power rather than the bristles of a brush. The airbrush was actually developed over 60 years ago and marketed for artists and process printing workers. It can be set to very fine standards so was used for touching up photographs as well as for drawing original artwork.

It had obvious uses for modellers, but for model aircraft amateurs the airbrush used to represent a very high investment. It needed a

16 Here are two airbrushes from the more expensive end of the market, in this case De Villbis Aerograph models. The principal is the same as in cheaper models but there is a pressure control on the propellants and the brushes have a wider range of nozzle adjustment and can produce a very fine line of paint if required. The airbrush on the left has a small paint reservoir within the barrel while the model on the right has a high volume reservoir, the spherical attachment. These airbrush equipments cost in Britain about £20 each (around $50). Two different sizes of propellant 'bomb' are also illustrated.

motorized compressor pump to provide the power, and the airbrush unit itself was expensive. In recent years this has changed considerably and now there is a wide range of different airbrush models at prices to suit most pockets. In America and elsewhere the use of an airbrush for model painting extends back some years, but in Britain the widespread adoption of the technique dates back only a few years when airbrush equipment makers produced sets and accessories suitable for model painting.

What has made the airbrush more viable as an investment for modellers is its new found portability. Instead of a compressor unit, an aerosol 'bomb' is provided to provide the power for the brush and though this has a strictly limited 'life' it is quickly replaceable at a relatively modest cost.

In very simple terms the airbrush is a fountain-pen like instrument with a fine air tube in it passing to a fine nozzle which is often (but not always) adjustable. A reservoir for the paint is incorporated, either within the brush or attached to it. An air tube connects to the aerosol 'bomb'. The aerosol unit sometimes has a control valve to limit its pressure, though not in cheap sets. Switching on the air supply sends the air under pressure through the airbrush and the venturi effect as it passes the paint reservoir pulls on the paint to emit it in a fine spray. Among models available are those by Badger, De Villbis (Aerograph), and Paabst. Some examples are shown here as is a typical set-up for using it.

Painting with the Airbrush

Painting with the airbrush (or indeed just with brushes) demands certain procedures to be observed, partly for safety, partly for good results, and partly to preserve domestic peace.

I must stress here that my own observations are based on the use of the De Villbis Aerograph. Less expensive models may have limitations which the Aerograph overcomes. However, practice on old discarded models, scrap parts, or plastic card sheets will quickly show you what your particular model of airbrush can or cannot do. Certainly do not try to paint a completed model until you have had a good practice session to familiarize yourself with the equipment.

In theory a practised operator could use an airbrush in the living room provided plenty of paper was put down on the table. This is not commended, however, and it is more usual to work in a den, workroom, outhouse, or shed,

etc.; somewhere where you will not be disturbed and where this sort of activity is more acceptable. This point applies equally to brush painting, of course, though I find that this is usually tolerated indoors so long as good protection is given to adjacent furnishings.

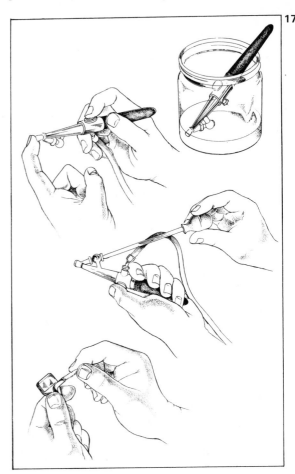

17 *(reading from top to bottom)* As a temporary measure to stop paint from drying and clogging the nozzle while you take a short break from spraying, leave the nozzle end immersed in thinners in a shallow jar. Blow through to clear the thinners before loading the reservoir with fresh paint.

If the airbrush clogs up it may have to be dissembled and cleaned to remove the offending particle. However, it can sometimes be cleared by placing the finger over the nozzle and switching on the air supply, which sometimes forces any particle into the paint reservoir where it can be seen and removed.

For temporary cleaning pour thinners into the paint reservoir, pipette fashion, and then shoot through with air, repeating as required until all the paint is cleared out.

At the end of a session the whole equipment should be dissembled and cleaned. A pipe-cleaner soaked in thinners is useful for cleaning out the paint reservoir.

Good ventilation is most essential to clear the paint fumes, another point applying equally to brush painting. When you clean your brushes or equipment, in particular, there will be vapour in the air. So keep an outside door or window open and stay alert to a possible build-up of fumes.

The maker's instructions for the use of air-brushes state that the paint in the reservoir should be 'milky' in consistency. This is fine for commercial artwork where water-based poster paint or inks might be used. In most cases modellers will be using plastic enamels. These could be 'watered' down with thinners but I find that even after most vigorous stirring there is a tendency for the pressure of the airbrush to separate out the paint pigment and the thinners with dire results. In practice, however, I find that fresh enamels, straight from the tin after mixing can be applied direct from the reservoir, provided that no impurities or lumps are in the paint. The best rule is to load little and often. When you see paint round the nozzle beginning to dry out then simply add a little more fresh paint and continue spraying. With the Aero-graph, even colour changing is simple. When one colour is sprayed out simply put the second colour into the reservoir and spray on to scrap plastic or your work surface until the second colour comes out strongly and cleanly. If time is at a premium, incidentally, it is worth planning your modelling programme so that two or more models are ready for one painting session destined for similar colour schemes, or at least with the main colour in common.

Having covered the basic principles of the use of the airbrush, let me reiterate here that an airbrush is *not* an essential for painting model aircraft, but used with skill it can enable you to get a superb finish on your models. Of course, you should study all the maker's literature and instructions relevant to the airbrush model you buy.

Masking

Whether you paint your model entirely by brush or mainly by airbrush you obviously have to face the fact that most aircraft are multi-coloured. Warplanes may be camouflaged or they may be drab above and light below, with various tactical markings in addition. Civil aircraft are usually brightly coloured with horizontal divisions and all manner of unusual paint adornments. A very skilled signwriter could, no doubt, paint a model entirely freehand. Most of us, however, have no such proficiency. A camouflaged aircraft with an irregular pattern of paint application lends itself to free-hand brush painting, but for straight or regular edge patterns, masking off the requisite areas is the easy way to do it.

18

18 The areas to be masked off for painting on this model are the anti-dazzle area (to be black) along the top of the nose and the yellow tailband and wing leading edges. Care is needed when applying the adhesive tape to get its edge exactly in the correct position. Rub down the tape gently but smoothly so that there is no tendency for the edges to lift. When applying the paint do not allow it to build up and form a ridge against the edge of the tape.

19

19 Here the adhesive tape has been peeled off to leave clean straight edges on the masked off area. Use tweezers to lift the tape. If any paint comes away with the tape (it rarely does if properly applied) retouch with the appropriate colour. This is Revell's Frank (Hayate) Japanese fighter.

You need ordinary self-adhesive clear tape and the only other requirement is to ensure that the basic colours of the model have been allowed to dry thoroughly overnight before any tape is applied.

The principles shown here apply to any type of painting where regular shapes are needed. For instance the black/white recognition stripes used on Allied aircraft in the 1944 period simply involves masking off and painting a solid white area, then masking out the white stripe portions and painting the whole lot over in black. When the masking tapes are removed a pattern of alternate white and black stripes is the result. Dazzle panels, tactical bands, tactical symbols (e.g., a diamond shape), and squadron colours in check or segment form can all be painted by masking out the required areas.

Also available is a jelly-like masking medium sold under several types of brand name, 'Maskol' being one of the most familiar. This is brushed over the area to be masked off and, in effect, it takes over the role of the adhesive tape. When painting is completed and the paint is dry, the masking agent peels or rubs off. 'Maskol' is specially useful for masking out airliner cabin windows, cockpit canopies, and other small awkwardly shaped parts which would be difficult to cover with adhesive tape. Sold in most countries is masking film; one brand I use is called 'Frisk Film'. This works just like ordinary adhesive tape but it has the advantage of being much softer and gentler and it comes with a backing sheet which allows it to be kept for re-use later. It can, of course, be cut with knife or scissors to any desired shape.

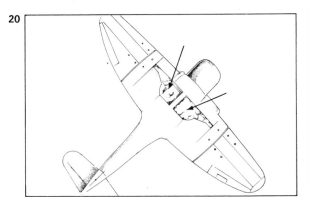

20 When airbrushing use wet domestic tissues to mask off the insides of wheel wells and bomb bays, etc, which may already have been painted in interior colours during assembly.

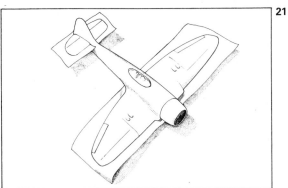

21 To mask off undersides when airbrushing use ordinary commercial masking tape. Note that here the cockpit is also padded out with tissue, having been painted and detailed before assembly of the model.

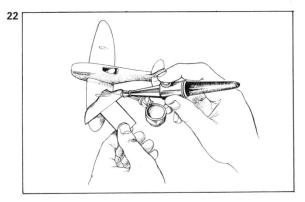

22 When airbrushing a camouflage finish the job can be speeded up considerably by cutting suitably shaped masking templates from thin card to match the patterns required. The template is simply held in position and the airbrush sprays round the edges. Actually this duplicates the way of masking off full-size aircraft. A 'feathered'

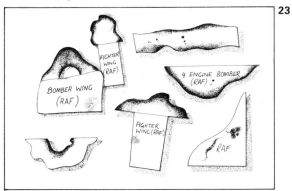

demarcation line results if the template is held just clear of the surface.

23 A selection of masking templates, each one marked so that it can be used over again when required.

Handling while Painting

It is, of course, necessary to move a model several times during painting, but try to work so as to reduce handling to a minimum. It is usual to keep one wingtip area until last so that the model can be handled from this tip only, while the rest of, say, the upper surface is painted. Then the model is put on a stand of some sort and the wingtip area can be painted last of all.

Dust is an enemy of the model painter, particularly the brush painter. Tiny particles can be imbedded in the drying paint and spoil an otherwise immaculate surface, though with modern quick drying paints it is not so much of a problem. Try to work in as dust free an environ-

ment as possible. Bedrooms are often dusty, due to frequent bed-making so I find other rooms better for this work. Slightly damp well ventilated rooms seem to offer the least amount of dust floating around in the air. As an added precaution while a model dries I find it a good idea to get a large open box (again a shoebox or something bigger) and punch some ventilation holes in the sides and ends. When painting is complete, carefully cover up the model with the box while the paint dries. Put any model well clear of small children or domestic pets while it dries, preferably on a high shelf.

Metal Finishes

I have already mentioned silver paint as a way of depicting a metal or unpainted surface. There are several alternatives to paint and they give a vastly superior finish if properly applied.

A few kits have appeared where the plastic parts themselves have been given a realistic plated finish which is most effective. These models are assembled like any other kit except that it is necessary to scrape away the plating from any edges which are to be cemented, since the plating is impervious to plastic cement. Special care is therefore needed to ensure careful assembly without ruining areas of plating adjacent to join lines. Cleaning up of joins must be carefully done and it will be necessary to use a little silver paint to touch out any noticeable

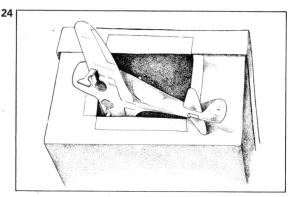

24 An old shoe box, or something a little smaller can make a convenient painting stand. Cut a hole in one end so that a wing can be placed into the stand. This is specially useful for airbrush painting. Any surplus paint goes into the box. Reinforce all edges with masking tape. Points of contact with the model are minimal and the box can be moved (carefully!) with the model *in situ* while the paint dries.

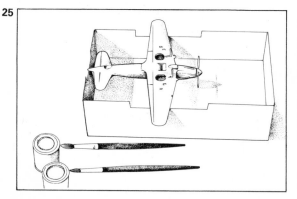

25 A variation that is more suitable for brush painting is a shoebox (or similar) with cut out sections in each rim to hold the wings or tail, etc. The model can be supported either way up while upper and lower surfaces are painted in turn. Have various size boxes available to suit several sizes of model.

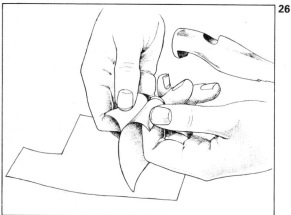

26 Metalskin is relatively thick, and raised surface detail on a plastic model must first be rubbed down to give a very smooth surface. The model is completed in the form of major sub-assemblies (wings, fuselage, etc). Individual Metalskin panels of convenient size are measured and cut from a large sheet. Rivet and panel detail is scribed into the Metalskin after all rubbing down is completed. Some form of pricker (or the teeth of a razor saw) is used to depict the lines of rivets.

join lines after assembly.

One old method of depicting a metallic finish was to use ordinary domestic cooking foil. Areas for wing panels, fuselage panels, and so on were carefully cut to shape, with a margin left over for trimming. Gloss varnish was applied to the areas to be covered, and the panels of foil were positioned and rubbed down over the model's surface detail when the varnish was in a semi-

dry state. After trimming and rubbing down the result could be most effective given a little practice at the art. This system can still be used but there are now at least two commercial ranges of self-adhesive foil finish on the market, 'Metalskin' and 'Baremetal'. The makers give extensive application instructions with these sheets but the diagrams here show how they are used.

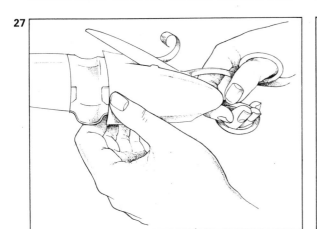

27 Flat areas, like wings, can be skinned in single large panels. Shown here is a typical wing with the overlap being trimmed off with scissors. The surfaces of the model must be scrupulously clean as any dust or dirt trapped under the Metalskin will show through as a 'bump' in the surface. Do not remove the Metalskin from its backing sheet until size and position of each respective panel has been checked.

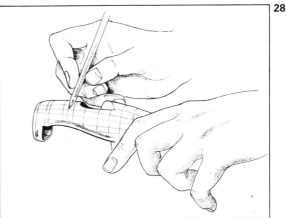

28 Here is a pricker being used to restore the surface detail after the Metalskin process is complete. Use a scale drawing as a guide to the surface detail, but failing that trace it from the kit parts before you begin the model.

29 A fine example of a model with Metalskin finish. This is the Rareplanes version of the Fury (now out of production) but the Matchbox model of the same aircraft can be similarly finished. Note that Metalskin is used here only to simulate the metal covered surfaces of the real machine – in this case

the forward fuselage and wheel covers, etc. Rest of the aircraft was silver doped, depicted by silver paint on the model. Note how the compound curves on the nose are achieved by cutting the Metalskin into small individual panels.

There remains one other material sometimes used to depict natural metal finish. This is a handicraft product sold as 'Rub'n'Buff' which comes in gold or silver shades, among others. The silver item is used. It is applied with a rubbing action like metal cleaner, left to set on the plastic surface, then buffed up with a cloth to give a high metallic gleam. Though I have used this in the past it does not seem to be quite so frequently used these days by model aircraft makers, but it is well worth trying.

Decals and Markings

Aside from the dramatic box-lid picture (usually an impression of the real aircraft), the next most colourful item in the kit is usually the decal sheet containing the markings for the model. These decals come in waterslide form and the design is printed on a solvent covered sheet and sealed by a varnish covering. When the sheet is soaked in water the solvent dissolves and the individual pieces can be slid from the sheet on

30 Baremetal differs from Metalskin in being very thin, rather like cigarette paper. Thus is can be applied directly over surface detail, which shows through the covering provided that it is properly rubbed down. This is well shown on Italaeri's 1:72 scale Thunderflash. All surface detail visible here is moulded into the plastic of the model. Baremetal has a short storage life and should be used as soon as possible after purchase.

31 Hasegawa's F-101C Voodoo treated with Baremetal. As with Metalskin it is best to make the model up into major sub-assemblies and cover these individually before final assembly. Clean surface is essential as dust or particles will show prominently through the covering (Baremetal).

to the appropriate part of the model. The sheet is normally cut into individual pieces first since each marking is applied in turn. Soaking the whole sheet would simply release all the markings together, sooner than they could be applied!

The kit box or instruction sheet usually gives a decal positioning guide and colour scheme drawing or description. Until about a decade ago, decals provided in kits were notoriously bad, or at best indifferent. Rarely did a kit maker come up with any very interesting or specific colour scheme or markings, often depending on over-familiar subjects. Corners were cut to keep the price down; for instance serial numbers would be printed in dark blue rather than black so that they could be printed together with the blue of national markings; or pale grey code letters might appear as white for simplicity on a decal sheet. Some of these old kits are still available, but the preliminary research you will be doing should enable you to pick out offenders in this respect, and the markings can be corrected by your own efforts. Similarly, some colour scheme details were given incorrectly in older kits and this is another thing to watch for.

Most modellers soon have a yearning to finish a model in different markings from those supplied in the kit. This has led to the production by small specialist firms of high quality decal sheets, often with much useful colour scheme information included, which can be used as an alternative to the markings supplied with the kit. Because these specialist sheets are short run items the price often exceeds that of the kit, but most enthusiasts accept this as fair value for the enhanced quality it gives to a model. Most sheets sold do, in fact, offer markings for three or more models all on the one sheet.

32 The more discerning standards of enthusiasts have, in recent years, led to big improvements in the decals and colour scheme details given with kits. Typical of modern standards are the markings provided with the Airfix Douglas Devastator. Note painted canopy framing (J. Groeneveld).

33 Here is a typical high quality decal sheet made by Modeldecal, a leading British producer in this field. The sheet provides decals and references for application to Frog's Buccaneer S.2. The model itself is shown finished in the actual markings for No 809 Sqn, Fleet Air Arm, supplied on the Modeldecal sheet. A second set of markings for a different aircraft comes on the same sheet. Also visible here are the reference details supplied with the decals. Original kit contained RAF and SAAF markings (Keith Palmer).

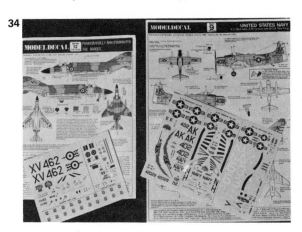

34 Two more typical Modeldecal sheets. The reference sheet containing full marking and colour scheme details is a very comprehensive production and a valuable adjunct to the markings themselves (Bryan Philpott).

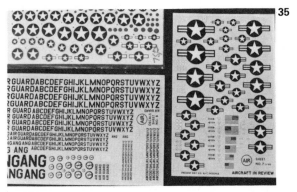

35 Apart from specialist decal sheets for individual aircraft it is also possible to obtain general sheets of useful decals. These three by the American firm of AIR cover United States insignia for various periods. Sheet on the right is for 1:48 while the others are 1:72 scale. The latter scale is by far the best catered for in the decal market (Bryan Philpott).

Dry Transfers

A major advance in recent years has been the advent of the 'dry transfer' produced by Letraset, or under the Letraset patents. A pressure sensitive design is provided on a backing paper and the marking is transferred to the model by rubbing it down into position from the backing sheet – a ball-pen is used for this. Availability varies from country to country and there are various trade names to look for, such as 'Squadron' (USA) and 'Dri-Dec' (Britain). Check advertisements in current hobby magazines for availability of all specialist decal sheets of any kind, since many are 'short run' productions and new releases are frequent.

Working with Dry Transfers

Aside from specialist dry transfers, quite a few of the commercial ranges of Letraset or similar products are of value to the modeller. The Blick firm, for instance, produce sheets of small miscellaneous lettering for modellers and the sheets include discs and lining and several colours are available. For such things as serials and work numbers the dry transfer sheets go down to letters and figures as small as 1/16 inch deep. Other dry transfer sheets provide discs of various sizes, ideal for camera ports, observation ports, gun ports, and so on, while others offer dashes and dots ideal for open exhaust ports or cartridge case ejector slots. For example the exhaust ports shown on the Fury model on page 61 are made from dashes from a Letraset sheet. Cheat lines, walkways, tactical signs, recognition stripes, code letters, and many other markings can be applied or adapted from dry transfer sheets.

Application of this sort of transfer can pose problems. With a waterslide decal the marking can be moved about slightly with a brush to get it into the precise position. With a dry transfer the application has to be correct first time. If it is wrongly placed the only course open is to carefully scrape it off and try again with a fresh transfer. This can be costly. I always mark the precise position with a pencil. Usually the transfer conceals the mark, but if it remains visible it can always be touched out with a spot of paint. More problems arise, however, when the marking has to be applied on a curved surface, under a tail, or in some other awkward spot. My usual procedure here is to cut out each individual letter in turn from the sheet with as big a surrounding area as possible. Small slivers

of adhesive tape are then cut to hold the individual letter in its precise position (either at the top and bottom edges or the sides) while the rubbing down of the transfer takes place. This is time consuming, but pays off by precise results. On an accessible but sharply curved surface it is possible to 'pre-transfer' the marking to some extent by loosening it by rubbing it down on the backing paper; then when the marking is placed in position only a light touch with a ball-pen is usually necessary to loosen the transfer and position it on the surface of the model.

With very small intricate serials and legends, another idea is to obtain a piece of clear waterslide decal (cut from the edge of a waterslide sheet), then make up the desired marking on the waterslide sheet, trim it, and apply it as a waterslide decal. This is much easier than trying to line up, say, the serial of a 1:144 scale model under its tailplane.

Using Waterslide Decals

Waterslide decals differ again in application. A golden rule which *must* be observed is to trim each and every subject close up to its edge. Each item on a waterslide sheet has a varnish covering which is inevitably slightly larger than the design it covers. Thus when applied there is a border of clear varnish surrounding each roundel and symbol; over paintwork this reflects the light and is an instant 'give away' which reveals the marking to be a decal rather than a painted item as it usually is on a real aircraft. With very small items, like serial markings, it is clearly impossible to cut out each individual tiny digit, but even this sort of marking can be cut close up to the top, bottom, and sides of the group of digits. In the case of larger letters or numbers it is usually possible to cut out each individual piece, but the centres of letters or numbers like 'Q' or '2' would normally be left intact.

Most modern waterslide decals behave well, can be moved into position as desired on the model, and will adhere well. If a decal cracks while it is in the water, fish out each piece on a sheet of glossy card, having let the pieces float off the backing. Then apply each piece of the decal as though it were a normal decal and position the pieces together *in situ*, jigsaw-puzzle fashion. If a decal folds up on itself while being applied, or sticks itself to your thumb, float it off into the saucer of water you are using, cut a piece of glossy card, and retrieve the decal flat (it should open out again in the water), and apply all over again. Some decals lose their adhesive properties after a second sojourn in the water and if any decal shows a tendency to lift or peel, leave it to dry, then place a fine smear of white PVA glue under the decal by careful application with a pin, taking care to use the glue so sparingly that none gets on adjacent painted surfaces or oozes out from under the decal.

Work each decal down with either blotting paper or a soft cloth so that it forms itself closely over any surface detail. Failure to do this could result in ugly air bubbles being left, or ridges forming against panel lines. Very often a model is painted over with clear matt (or semi-matt) varnish after painting (or sprayed with Testor's 'Dulcote' or 'Gloscote') and this helps seal the decal completely against any cracking or peeling at a later date. Even if the model itself is not varnished all over, however, it is worth carefully varnishing over each decal to seal it, taking care not to run the varnish out over adjacent paintwork.

Using Spare Decals

Many kits offer spare or optional markings – e.g. when a choice of colour schemes is given – so in no time at all you start to generate a collection of oddments, all of which can be hoarded for future use. Keep all offcuts too, as all will come in handy at some future time allowing you to come up with marking schemes derived from your own research efforts and quite original to your own models.

36 Here is a good example of an aircraft in a 'different' colour scheme which could easily be depicted in model form. This ex-Luftwaffe Fieseler Storch was captured by the RAF and is seen in British service in 1946. It is painted silver overall with black propeller. Airfix produce a 1:72 scale kit and you can simply make this up, find six RAF roundels and suitable letters for the serial numbers, plus a fin flash, and apply. The Luftwaffe decals supplied in the kit can then go into your spare decal stock where they will come in useful on some subsequent project (C. Holland *via* L. Hunt).

As your collection of spare decals grows you need somewhere to store them. Folders or envelopes are suitable, but I prefer one of those modern picture albums with clear wallets as a 'de luxe' storage system where the decals can be kept clean and flat and availability can be discovered at a glance. The wallets allow the marking to be segregated by type and country as the stock increases.

One last point worth considering is 'decal sharing'. Specialist decals, and large Letraset dry transfer sheets can be expensive. A group of friends who were all model aircraft enthusiasts could buy one sheet between them and so spread the cost.

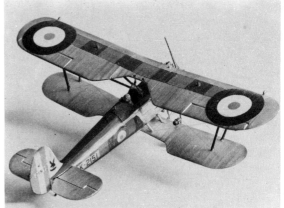

37

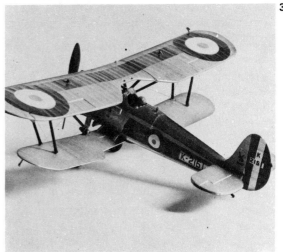

38

37–38 A good example of 'home-made' markings is shown on this Airfix 1:72 scale Bristol Bulldog. The roundels are from the kit but the tail stripes are hand-painted, as are the red/blue squadron colours, all using the adhesive tape masking techniques previously described. The serial number was obtained by cutting up and re-arranging the kit serials. The squadron badge was hand-painted using a very fine brush (Mike Gething).

39 This 1:48 scale Grumman Gulfhawk from a Monogram kit uses the kit decals with added markings from other sources. Name on fin and engine is from Blick, and the tiny stencil marks are hand-painted using a fine brush (and a steady hand!). All supplement the kit decals. As a civil high performance machine this aircraft has a gloss finish. Gloss paint sold in hobby shops is too gloss so the model was painted matt, the decals were positioned, then the entire model was given a coat of semi-gloss varnish (Roy Williams).

Wear and Weathering

To complete the all important subject of model finishing we must look at the most difficult of all effects to achieve – the used look. Few aircraft stay pristine and fresh for very long. In combat or service use aircraft soon take on a very worn appearance, sometimes even becoming quite battered in the process.

Paint wears away from leading edges or is scuffed off by maintenance men working on the wings, etc. Exhaust stains and oil leaks appear, mud or sand is thrown up on landing or take-off. Damage is patched or covered in fresh paint and aircraft operating over the sea get distinctly salt stained and faded. Code letters and other markings are replaced or painted out, marking styles are changed temporarily, and so on. All have their effect on appearance. At the beginning of this section I suggested toning down basic colours a little as a step towards getting a worn look. If you do not overdo it, all other weathering and wear effects can be achieved with brush or airbrush work. Some of the colour pictures in the book show what can be achieved in this respect, and the following pictures give more good examples.

40 Revell Hayate after completion has had its skinning given a very worn and weathered look by rubbing a little graphite over the wings and fuselage on the tips of the fingers. This picks out the panelling and rivet lines and gives prominence to the frame sections etc., characteristic of many 'war weary' aircraft in the 1944–45 period.

41 Extremely battered and weathered Airfix 1:72 scale Catalina has been given a very salt stained and paint worn appearance based on pictures of the real thing. Paint was toned down as previously described and the various patches of bare metal showing through the paint were applied on the 'dry brush' principle using a small brush. Dribbles and stains were applied the same way.

42 Airfix 1:72 scale Grumman Hellcat with typical wear and weathering for a naval aircraft. This being a dark blue model the exhaust staining was made greyish brown and in this case has been applied by airbrush. Wear to bare metal on the wing ammunition hatches has in this case been indicated with a touch of 'Rub'n'Buff' (Jerry Scutts).

43 Frog 1:72 scale Hellcat in faded slate grey and sea green, standard 1944 Fleet Air Arm finish. Darker exhaust staining is used here, and weather streaking has been subtly applied over wings and tailplanes and upper fuselage areas to simulate the effect of rain and salt spray blowing over the aircraft while on a carrier's deck in bad weather. A dark wash run into aileron, elevator, and rudder hinge lines, emphasizes the control surfaces well by providing artificial shadow, and this latter technique can be used to advantage on almost any aircraft model. Use thinners and black or dark grey paint for this wash and apply it very sparingly (Jerry Scutts).

8: More Advanced Models

Most present-day aircraft modellers are quite happy to stay with plastic kits, for the number of available kits is enormous and the flow of new releases is enough to keep the average enthusiast working at full stretch. However, you may well wish to savour something different, or make a model not yet produced in plastic kit form.

One alternative is to turn the clock back to pre-plastic kit days and make models from wood, either balsa wood or harder varieties. This sort of model is literally carved out of a wood block which has been cut to rough overall scale dimensions. A good scale plan is needed, complete with cross-sections, and card templates are made up to check fuselage and wing outlines and contours as you proceed. Quite a few modellers still work in this material and one or two samples are shown, one by Peter Halliday, a leading exponent of the art today.

1 Typical of an aircraft type not issued in kit form but built from scratch in wood is this fine Supermarine 535 made by a member of the Shuttleworth Trust Supporters Association. It is 1:72 scale and the cockpit canopy is moulded from acetate in the way shown in chapter 4 of this book.

2 At the other end of the scratch-building spectrum comes this magnificent Supermarine Sea Eagle of 1923 vintage built by Peter Halliday for British Airways and presented to the States of Guernsey in 1973 to commemorate 50 years of flying between England and the Channel Islands. Note use of wire for detailing. Rigging is of fine thread (Peter Halliday/British Airways).

An alternative to wood, and now much more widely used for scratch-building is plastic card. Building model aircraft from this material is really an art in itself with its own techniques. Essentially, however, models made from plastic card are usually fabricated in sub-assemblies, often following the style of the real aircraft. The internal framing is usually simplified and adapted, but externally fine scale fidelity is paramount. Actual assembly methods depend on the aircraft type, but the use of a wood 'girder' as mainspar is common. Several model magazines from time to time carry articles dealing in detail with the construction of specific aircraft models in plastic card.

3 This big Hamilcar glider of 1944 vintage is built entirely from plastic card. As scratch-built models go it is one of the easier subjects, having a box-like fuselage and plain rectangular wings and tail. The nose is hinged to open as on the real aircraft and the interior is detailed with stringers and framing, while a miniature tank can be carried on as the real thing (Michael Moore).

For those who wish to progress from plastic kits without getting involved in the intricacies of scratch-building, there is a further alternative which has appeared in recent years. This is the vacuum-formed (or vac-form) kit. In effect this fills the gap between conventional plastic kits and scratch building in plastic card, combining techniques from the two. The vac-form kit consists of a thick styrene or PVC sheet moulded to give a set of shaped parts which can be cut from the sheet and assembled on fairly conventional lines. Firms in this business include Rareplanes, Warbirds, Skyframes, and Airmodel. These are mostly small concerns who produce runs of as little as 500 samples of a given kit, this being possible because vac-forming is a relatively cheap process compared with the immense expense involved in tooling for injection-moulded plastic kits. Vac-forms are intended solely for enthusiasts and the subjects are often

replicas of true rarities which would not, in any case, have sufficient commercial appeal for any of the big kit makers to mass produce.

Vac-form kits are not for beginners, but anyone with some years of kit building experience should be able to make them up. They demand much more time and skill than a conventional kit, though instructions and drawings are supplied.

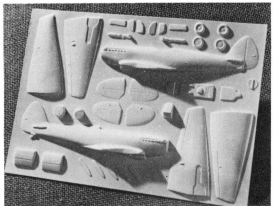

4 A typical vac-form kit, in this case for the Supermarine Spiteful, a short-lived successor to the Spitfire. Every component is moulded on the sheet but in practice it is usual to utilize as many small parts as possible from the contents of the modeller's spares box. Wheels, propellers, and other parts would be cannibalized from other kits where possible (Rareplanes).

5 The parts are cut out clear of the actual outline, then carefully sanded down to exact profile, and adjoining parts are constantly matched to ensure a good join. Extreme care is necessary for a false move could damage the rather thin plastic or cause distortion. The value of a good flat worktop (in this case Formica) is apparent here. Use a circular motion to sand down the parts to fit, thus ensuring even reduction (Rareplanes).

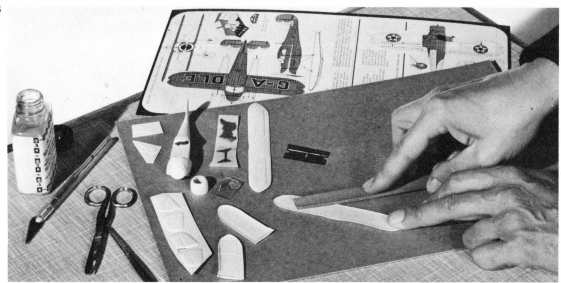

6 When the fuselage halves make a good butt join, carefully tape them together, then run Mekpak or similar into the join with a brush. On PVC moulded samples use PVC cement or universal type glues. To reinforce the join, the makers commend plastic card strips cemented under one of the butting edges. While the fuselage is setting, similar treatment is given to the wings. At least one maker produces vac-form kits from a central 'core' section to which the outside halves and panels are cemented, making for a rigid structure. Extreme care is needed with the wings, especially in getting the correct dihedral. For biplane models the interplane struts, though supplied with the kit in vac-form style, are best replaced with struts from the spares box or made from plastic card strip (Rareplanes).

7 Typical of the more exotic types available in vac-form style is this Bell Airacuda, one of the biggest Rareplanes kits. Strips of tape (in this case silver coated tape) are used on this model for the canopy framing. The rest of the model is covered with Metalskin (Rareplanes).

8 If you are a beginner at vac-form kits choose a simple subject first, like this Heinkel 112. As vac-form kits are usually short run items you may not find this actual Rareplanes kit available, but watch model magazine adverts to see what is current. Wheels and propeller on this model were taken from other kits. Decals are not supplied with the average vac-form kit (Rareplanes).

Finally, if you want something out of the run of all that has so far been described, remember that there is a reasonable selection of card cut-out model aircraft available. Most of those now produced are quite sophisticated, requiring a great deal of care and skill to complete. Poland, Czechoslovakia, East and West Germany, and Austria are major makers of this type of model. Within the limitations of the medium a surprisingly high standard has been achieved though these card models are really in a class by themselves with their own appeal. They do not really go with models made from wood, plastic, or plastic card.

9 Two card kits from Austria are shown here. To 1:33 scale, they are for a Beech Bonanza and a Focke Wulfe Fw 190A, both fully (and realistically) pre-coloured.

9: Display and Photography

Once you start to build up a collection of models – even three or four aircraft – you are faced with where to keep them safe and sound. Model aircraft of any kind are inherently fragile, with many vulnerable and delicate parts which are only too easily snapped off with clumsy handling. The beginner to modelling usually puts his models on a shelf and in these conditions they are most susceptible to damage. Also they will quickly acquire a layer of dust and will be liable to casual handling by anyone who might chance by. Display or storage can become a major problem which will partly depend on your own circumstances and financial resources for its resolution. Here, however, we can consider a few factors involved.

1. Dust and careless handling, twin problems, can be solved by putting the models under cover, preferably in some sort of display case. A handyman with carpentry experience will be

1 White-wood bookcase and kitchen cabinet converted to show cases. Turning the cabinet upside down (background) puts the widest shelf at the bottom, convenient for larger models.

able to make a proper showcase with sliding doors, and possibly with strip lighting inside. I have seen some excellent 'floor to ceiling' display cases made this way by the expedient of

shelving and glassing in alcoves or the space each side of a chimney breast. It is possible to get this sort of work done professionally, or to purchase purpose-built showcases, but the cost is very high in each case.

An alternative which I use myself is the glass-fronted type of 'utility' white-wood bookcase or kitchen cabinet of the type which comes unpainted. These have sliding doors and it is a simple enough matter to add extra shelves between the shelving already fitted in the unit. When painted these make a good fairly cheap form of showcase with a reasonably large capacity. The kitchen cabinet units can be wall-suspended or stood on top of other furniture if floor space is at a minimum.

A further alternative for a large display case is an old china or dresser cabinet. These can sometimes be obtained at 'junk yard' prices; when painted and renovated (perhaps with extra shelving added) they can look attractive.

Lastly there is a type of 'individual' showcase just big enough for a single model and available quite cheaply at leading hobby stores. They range from rigid plastic or Perspex construction to thin vac-formed types. Several small models will fit in the largest of these types. A very similar alternative is the transparent plastic food container which comes in a great range of sizes at many chain stores.

2. Enthusiasts without showcase facilities come up with all sorts of ways of keeping models out of harms way, albeit exposed to dust and other hazards. A common idea is to suspend the models overhead on lengths of cotton in 'action' formations. I do not like this arrangement though, as the cotton inevitably breaks at some time and the model concerned smashes to pieces on the floor; the cotton and the aircraft each gather dust and the whole lot soon becomes an eyesore. A more compact and secure idea which can be effective is to have the models on strong wire rods which radiate from a central

anchoring point, such as a well finished block of wood. This has to be heavy enough to keep the whole lot stable. And the display piece must be put somewhere where it will not be knocked over. Another idea is to group the models on pre-painted sheets of hardboard or pegboard, after which they can be secured to walls or other surfaces. For both these ideas you need to utilize either the slot provided in most models for the display stand, or a special hole will need to be drilled to take a securing peg or wire.

2 Display block arrangement for models.

2

3

3 Pegboard or hardboard display panels secured to wall or even ceilings. The complete photographic set-up described on page 75 is being arranged.

3. Dusting is needed weekly on models which are displayed in the open. Use a large soft paintbrush or a 'blower' type brush as supplied for ciné projectors. Take great care not to knock off small detail pieces while dusting. I find that even models kept in a display case need dusting occasionally, say twice a year at least.

4. Frequent maintenance is desirable to ensure that any damage sustained is repaired quickly. Loose broken pieces left lying around get lost all too easily.

5. It is better to store models which cannot be reasonably displayed. Shoeboxes and the like make good strong containers. Crumpled paper or pieces of plastic foam are very suitable for packing material, put loosely into each box around the model. Mark the box contents

clearly to aid quick location of any particular model when it is later required. Keep the boxes on a high shelf or better still in a cupboard. Many modellers build up a much bigger collection of models than they have room to display. If your display case has limited capacity it is a good idea to rotate your models between store and show using the periodic change-over for dusting and maintenance.

6. Available space could influence your choice of scale. For instance a student living in single room 'bed-sitter' accommodation might be better to work with 1:100 or 1:144 scales if a reasonably sized collection is needed. A single shoebox could hold as many as twelve 1:144 scale models.

7. Plastic models can be adversely affected by heat – too much of it can lead to warping, sagging, and fading. Avoid siting any display case near a radiator or a window. Similarly avoid the close proximity of light bulbs. Paint and decals can fade or discolour in strong sunlight.

Bear in mind that the foregoing remarks cover the subject of display and storage in a very broad way. This is a matter much affected by your own personal circumstances. I have met enthusiasts lucky enough to have a complete room lined with glass display cases, while others never aspire to more than a few shoeboxes full of models tucked into the corner of a cupboard.

A popular tendency in recent years has been to take over an idea once more common to the model soldier hobby. This is the diorama, or scenic setting, in which the model is displayed in appropriate surroundings. For instance a fighter plane of the Second World War might have been dispersed in a blast-protected bay at the airfield edge, and while at the ready for take-off it might have a starter battery trolley plugged into the engine, maintenance crew carrying out routine checks, armourers reloading the ammunition bays, and so on. A diorama of, say, a Spitfire, might duplicate all this in miniature, utilizing scale figures and equipment and model rail scenic accessories of the sort widely available in hobby stores. A small piece of wood, chipboard, or hardboard suffices for a base and there is a wide choice of treatment depending on the model or period depicted. There is no shortage of accessories. Airfix make numerous boxes of OO/HO figures suitable for 1:72 scale, there are N gauge figures (and trucks and stores) suitable for 1:144 scale, and cast metal or plastic figures for 1:32 or 1:24 scale. Hasegawa and Airfix make some actual airfield service vehicles.

4 Suitable pilot figures and other flying personnel are available in several scales. This 1:24 scale Series 77 RAF pilot of 1940, in cast metal, is intended to go with Airfix 1:24 scale aircraft models.

4

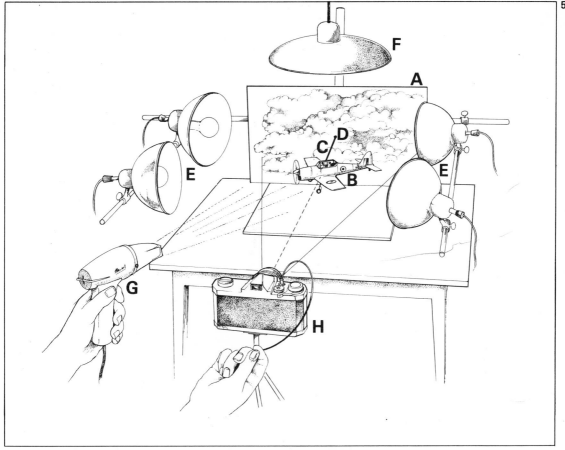

5 Equipment and set-up for taking a suggested flying shot of a plastic aircraft model. The model is clamped with thick rigid wire bent around one of the wings and fixed behind the background illustration on the vertical stand supporting it.
A. painted background plate or picture.
B. aircraft model.
C. thick rigid wire (brass).
D. hole in background.
E. four lamps with 75-watt bulbs

F. floodlight with 100-watt bulb.
G. hair-drier to turn prop
H. reflex camera on tripod.
Note the trick of using a hair-drier to turn the propeller and so get a convincing 'action' shot. If the model is suspended rigidly enough the drier can be dispensed with and a flick of the propeller with the finger, just before exposure, may suffice; however, great care must be taken not to vibrate the airplane.

Photography

Ownership of a camera is becoming more and more common at the present time, and it is becoming a popular pastime to attempt to photograph completed models in a realistic setting. Strictly speaking this is a subject for a practical photography book, but some slight coverage of model aircraft photography is appropriate here. If you have either a single lens reflex or twin lens reflex camera you will certainly have no trouble in taking pictures of models. For most cameras you will need either an extension tube or a 1 or 2 dioptre close-up lens attachment, but with some cameras with, say, an 80 mm/f2 lens, it is possible to focus as close as 17 inches with no need for close-up devices. For the average 1 : 72 scale model this is fine. With non-reflex cameras you will need to do some experimentation to overcome the problem of parallax and depth of field, both of which are no great problem with a reflex camera where the viewfinder shows you exactly what the camera sees. As a general rule maximum depth of field (i.e., the areas before the camera actually in focus) is achieved by using the smallest stop on the camera, usually f16 or f22. To compensate for this you use a relatively long exposure time, thus making a tripod and cable release a necessity. To show what can be achieved, given all

these basic requirements, I asked J. Groeneveld, who took a number of the photographs in this book, and who is a specialist in this art, to show us the typical arrangement which was needed to take the photographs.

Note that the same set-up is used for photographing aircraft 'on the ground' except, of course, that no wire support is needed. The 'ground' needs suitable scenic treatment, but at its simplest can be just a sheet of 'grass' paper as sold in hobby stores. Aircraft with undercarriages modelled in the 'down' position can be photographed in the air either by depicting take-off or landing situations, or by arranging them so that the undercarriage is hidden by the wings. Finally, model aircraft can be photographed for 'record purposes' against a plain background – either white or coloured. Some effective colour photography can be done here – for instance a silver aircraft photographed against a bright red background can make a 'pretty' picture in its own right.

6 Here is a close-up of the model supported on its rigid wire support. The loop which grips the wing will, of course, be hidden from the camera's 'view' (J. Groeneveld).

7 Here is the complete set-up seen from a little above the photographic angle, with all the lights in position. In summer it is possible to take this same sort of picture outdoors in good sunlight. White sheets can replace the lights each side of the model to act as reflectors and thus soften the shadows, and care is needed to get the position favourable in relation to the light source. (J. Groeneveld).

8 Here is a similar picture taken with the same set-up as is illustrated here. The Italaeri 1 : 72 scale Fiat Br 20 is shown. The shutter speed was 1/30 second at f11 and the background came from a travel poster. Travel posters, calendar illustrations, and the like make ideal backgrounds though anyone with artistic ability could paint his own (J. Groeneveld).

Appendix

Kit makers and accessory suppliers

The scale model aircraft hobby is served by hundreds of hobby stores world-wide, and many large department stores and chain stores also sell model kits and accessories. Stocks vary in degree from just a small selection of kits and paints to a truly comprehensive range which covers just about everything available at a given time. As the hobby is supported by a number of magazines and journals, current information on what is in production or on sale is best taken from up-to-date editions of any of these publications, all of which carry reviews and news of new items as well as advertisements from kit makers and suppliers. Kits and accessories do not necessarily remain in continuous supply (they are often withdrawn, re-issued, or revised) and there is always a flow of new items. Most of the 'brand names' in the model aircraft field will already be familiar to readers of this book, but distributors (and even trade-marks) can vary from country to country. Some of the principal 'names' to look for are given here. I have refrained from giving addresses, partly because they change, and partly because few kit and accessory makers deal directly with the public in any case – their products are sold through the retail trade.

1. *Plastic aircraft kit makers*
Great Britain Airfix, Frog, Revell (GB), Matchbox (Lesney Products)
United States of America Aurora, Hawk, Monogram, Lindbergh, Jo-han, Life-Like, Revell
France Heller
West Germany Faller, Airmodel

Czechoslovakia KP
Italy Artiplast, Avio-Modelli, Italaeri
East Germany (GDR) VEB, Kurthaufe
Japan Aosima, Eidai, Fujimi, Hasegawa, Nichimo, Nitto, Imai, Otaki, Revell (Japan), Tamiya
Poland Ruch
(NB The above are principal kit makers only – there are other smaller concerns with less widespread availability or very limited output.)

2. *Vac-form aircraft kit makers*
Great Britain Rareplanes, Sutcliffe
Canada Airframe
West Germany Airmodel

3. *Decal producers*
Great Britain Modeldecal, Dri-dec
Denmark Stoppel
United States of America AIR Decals, Microdecals, Squadron
West Germany Plasty
Italy ESCI
France Max-ABT
(NB The above are principal producers only – there are many other small producers with limited output and availability in the specialist decal field.)

4. *Kit distributors*
Great Britain RIKO (Richard Kohnstamm Ltd), A. A. Hales Ltd
West Germany Plasty
United States of America AHM (Associated Hobby Manufacturers), MPC, Squadron Shops
Austria Hobby-Sömmer
(NB The above are principal distributors mainly of imported kits in their respective countries. There are, however, many other firms acting as distributors.)

5. *Paint and accessory makers and suppliers*
Great Britain Humbrol, Joy, Airfix (paints and adhesives), Multicraft, Swann & Morton (knives and tools)
United States of America Pactra, Testor, Floqil (paints and adhesives), X-acto (knives and tools), Plastruct (plastic parts and accessories for general model use)
France Modelcolor (paint)
(NB The above products are widely distributed throughout various parts of the world. There are many other smaller producers in the accessory and paint business. Plastic card sheet and strip is also available under numerous brand names.)

Mail order
Even if you do not live near any good hobby kit supplier, there are many firms offering a mail order service. Most of these firms advertise in the major modelling magazines and they can usually supply just about anything that is currently available. When ordering by mail, take care to state quite clearly your name and address, the item(s) you require, any alternatives in lieu of first-choice items, and enclose the correct remittance together with any return postage or handling charge as stated in the dealer's advertisement. Confusion which sometimes arises in mail order transactions is often due to careless or casual ordering. Keep a record of any order placed or remittance value in case you need to make any claims for non-arrival of goods ordered.

Index

ORISKANY HIGH SCHOOL LIBRARY

ORISKANY, NEW YORK